LIVERPOOL HEROES

Book 1

The stories of 16 Liverpool holders of the Victoria Cross

Best wishes.

Bill Sergeant

Edited by Ann Clayton

Researched by
Sid Lindsay
Bill Sergeant
and Ann Clayton

2006

First published in Great Britain in 2006 by the

NOEL CHAVASSE VC MEMORIAL ASSOCIATION
Registered Charity No. 1112413

Copyright NCVCMA 2006
ISBN 0-9553495-0-8
978-0-9553495-0-8

All proceeds from the sale of this book will go towards the funding of a
Victoria Cross Memorial Statue in the City of Liverpool

Further copies, price £7.00 + p&p may be obtained from:

DONALD ALLERSTON
12 WEXFORD AVENUE
HALE VILLAGE
MERSEYSIDE L24 5RY
UNITED KINGDOM

Printed by Printstat, St. Helens, Merseyside, WA10 2PF, United Kingdom

Contents

Foreword
by
Bill Sergeant

As a youngster attending Everton Road Methodist Church, I well remember learning a quotation from John 15.13: 'Greater love hath no man than this, that a man lay down his life for his friends'. At the time, I thought the quotation related only to the sacrifice made by our Lord Jesus Christ. Over the years, I have come to appreciate that many of our recent predecessors made exactly that sacrifice in world conflicts, especially in the two world wars. In recent visits to the Western Front war cemeteries, I have read versions of this quotation on many headstones, most notably on that of Noel Godfrey Chavasse, VC and Bar, MC at Brandhoek near Ypres in Belgium. Having spent some time reading about Chavasse's early life and family upbringing, I feel that I might be forgiven for drawing such a comparison between Our Lord and those brave men and women who made the same sacrifice for mankind.

I visit the Western Front to pay my respects to those to whom we owe our present-day freedom and in particular to visit the graves and memorials of the bravest of men – those who were awarded the Victoria Cross. I suppose my interest in Victoria Cross holders began about five years ago when I visited the grave of my recently deceased wife, and whilst wandering around Allerton Cemetery, Liverpool, I came across the name of George Edward NURSE, VC who died in 1947. By gaining access to some unpublished research by Sid Lindsay from Aigburth, I found that Nurse had actually been awarded his VC in December 1899 at Colenso, during the Boer War. He had been born in Northern Ireland, moved to Liverpool, serving in and surviving not only the Boer War but also the Great War, and eventually died in Liverpool in comparative obscurity. Through Sid's notes, I also found in Allerton Cemetery the grave of William Ratcliffe VC, a Liverpool docker who had served in the South African war before being awarded a Military Medal at Messines in April 1917, and a Victoria Cross at the same place some seven weeks later. Ratcliffe also survived the Great War, dying in Liverpool in 1963, again in relative obscurity. I subsequently discussed with Sid the possibility of having his research published as a series of small books, thus making some contribution to raising awareness of the existence and deeds of these Heroes and perhaps ensuring that their names would survive the passage of time.

Unfortunately, Sid suffered from considerable ill health at about this time and did not have the energy to pursue this possibility himself. In fact, Sid passed away early in 2006. With the permission of his widow, Betty, and in collaboration with a mutual friend, Don Allerston, I decided to try to publish Sid's research. Sid was always the first to remind me that his research was incomplete and there were several gaps in the many biographical notes he had compiled. For instance, he had discovered 14 holders of the Victoria Cross who he believed were actually born in Liverpool. By chance, I found a 15th (H. M. McKenzie) who he had missed. Similarly, continued research by others has found that one or two presumptions made by Sid now need to be amended. What he and I had agreed, however, was that the first booklet should deal with those Liverpool-born VC holders, with subsequent publications dealing with, for example, those like George Nurse who were not born in Liverpool but spent most of their lives here and were Liverpool residents when they received their medals; or those who were born at addresses, for example Seaforth, Waterloo etc, which were not part of Liverpool at the time of their birth but were subsequently absorbed into Liverpool. In effect, there will probably need to be four or five separate volumes to do justice to Sid's research.

Don and I discussed the sad circumstances in which several of our 'Liverpool Heroes' later died, and with others of a like mind, especially local historian Dr Frank Carlyle, Chavasse's biographer Ann Clayton, and a group of friends from Hale Village, we decided to do something to rectify what we saw as a glaring failure by the City and residents of Liverpool – the absence of any memorial either to Noel Chavasse VC & Bar, or to any of the other VC winners with Liverpool connections. And this some 150 years after our first Liverpool VC was won! We decided as a group that we would assume responsibility for raising the necessary finance and for erecting a suitable memorial, not only to Noel Chavasse but also to the other 15 Liverpool-born VC holders. We formed the **Noel Chavasse VC Memorial Association (NCVCMA)** in July 2005 and set about raising the money. This was an ambitious plan, certainly, but one which we felt was capable of achievement, hopefully by early 2007. Our sculptor, Tom Murphy, has already produced a model of the memorial which has been seen by the Chavasse family, local historians, military associations etc.

All have expressed their satisfaction that the memorial, which will be in bronze and some 8 feet high, is in a traditional form. It will in fact depict Chavasse and a stretcher-bearer tending a wounded soldier on the battlefield. The life and deeds of Chavasse will be dealt with in detail later in this book but he earned all of his awards as a Medical Officer rescuing and treating his wounded comrades. The memorial is intended to illustrate Chavasse's devotion to his fellow men rather than any specific episode. Around the plinth of the memorial will be the names of the other 15 VC holders. To bring me back to my opening remarks and at the request of Noel Chavasse's nephew and family, the inscription on the memorial will include the quotation which is engraved on his headstone: *'Greater love hath no man than this, that a man lay down his life for his friends'.*

I and the other members of the NCVCVMA Committee hope that you will find the memorial itself inspirational and aesthetically pleasing and that this and subsequent booklets will help readers to better appreciate the valour and self-sacrifice of many of our 'Liverpool Heroes', thereby preserving their names and memories. The generous help given by numerous individuals and organisations in the preparation of this book is gratefully acknowledged by the Committee. Every effort has been made to trace and acknowledge the holders of copyright relating to the images reproduced here.

All proceeds from the sale of this book will go to the NCVCMA, Registered Charity No. 1112413, and will be used in accordance with our Objectives: to maintain the memorial and promote within local schools and communities an awareness of the debt owed by us all to these brave men.

Noel Chavasse VC Memorial Association

Chair:	William Sergeant QPM LLB
Secretary:	Marie Fisher
Treasurer:	Paul Bostock
Trustees:	Bill Sergeant, Don Allerston, Paul Bostock Dr Frank Carlyle, Marie Fisher, Jim Flannigan
Committee members:	Ann Clayton MA, Tony Davies, Bob Dunn, David Hudson, Joyce Hughes, George Main, George Poynton, Jim Ross

$\mathcal{I}$ntroduction
by
Sid Lindsay

[The notes upon which this Introduction is based were compiled by Sid Lindsay, whose work on local Victoria Cross heroes has inspired the production of this book. Sadly, Sid passed away without knowing that his findings, augmented by later research, were to be published. However, he did know that the final paragraph below was prophetic: a fifteenth Liverpool VC came to light recently, Lt Hugh McDonald McKenzie. Sid was delighted that this omission was to be rectified. W. Sergeant]

This collection of notes came about as a result of some private research I did into the businesses and trades of Merseyside. Whilst thus engaged, in 1986 I came across the name of Captain Gabriel George Coury VC, who with his family was involved in the Liverpool Cotton Trade. It then occurred to me that there was no record of local recipients of the Victoria Cross in one collection, and I decided to attempt to rectify this omission. I naively believed that the lives of such heroes would be well-documented and that all I would need to do was to draw up a list of names and quickly gather together the stories of their deeds and lives.

I began with an initial list of 20 names but this number soon rose to 62, some admittedly having only a slight connection with Merseyside. I had not anticipated that for many of these heroes there was little on record other than birth, death and citation. To my disappointment I quickly found that the most likely sources, such as Regimental Associations and Museums and the Royal British Legion were not the best informed and in some instances, sadly, seemed to be uninterested. As a mere novice in such matters, this lack of response caused me considerable frustration and meant that the project took much longer than I had anticipated.

I am not a military historian, nor am I a proficient storyteller. Consequently, this is simply meant to be a collection of biographical notes about some very special people. Inevitably, there will be mistakes due to my lack of expertise. I have made many errors while researching, but each has served only to make me seek another direction to find out what I needed to know. Compared to the depth of research which goes into the writing of some of the major tomes to which I have had access, my task has been of a comparatively short duration. Nevertheless it has tested my patience, as well as that of my longsuffering wife, Betty, to the limits. It has made me realise, above all, how important it is that similar exercises are undertaken to ensure that other aspects of our local history are recorded for posterity. I urge anybody who can do so to make their contribution by jotting down notes on their own lives, their family history, the firm for which they work or worked, military and public service or just memories of things that used to be. Otherwise, as with my gallant subjects, this information will be lost. Believe me, the satisfaction to be gained is considerable.

My enquiries have brought me into contact with many correspondents who share my interest in the lives of these heroic figures, awarded the nation's highest accolade for conspicuous bravery. I am truly indebted to these kind and considerate people who took the time and trouble to write to me offering valuable help and words of encouragement. I have to confess that not until this late stage of my life have I had any real knowledge of these brave men and their deeds. Like many of my contemporaries, I took such valour for granted. However, if this belated attempt at paying homage helps ensure a continuing interest in the lives of the recipients, or arouses or revives interest in other seemingly forgotten heroes, then my work will have been worthwhile.

There has been a temptation from time to time to compare one Victoria Cross deed with another, a temptation which I have tried to resist. In my somewhat elementary researches, I have been generally and genuinely appalled by the horrors which have been perpetrated and endured in the service of one's country. I am also conscious that the holders of the Victoria Cross are the selected representatives of many, many more very brave men and women who gave their all in their country's cause. I have no wish to demean the achievements of those who hold the Cross, but I feel certain that our heroes would never want us to forget their many colleagues who deserved to be recognised as much as or even more than they themselves, had fate or circumstance so decreed. My own active service was of little consequence – I was called up early in 1945 and spent most of my time in Italy, serving with the Royal Electrical and Mechanical Engineers until 1948.

Reading the numerous accounts of these great men, I constantly felt personally involved in the events that surrounded them: the great sacrifices made, the sweethearts, wives, children and parents whose pride was so severely tempered by poignant loss. I was also struck by the many mysteries with which some of our heroes surrounded themselves almost like a shield against the 'fame' attracted by their achievements. How sad it was that so many of them were eventually to leave this world friendless and almost forgotten.

I hope that these notes will be read with interest. I hope that my list is complete, but would not be surprised to learn that there are more Liverpool-born heroes than the 14 I have identified. We have good cause to be grateful to every one of them, for it is to them and their companions that we owe the quality of life which we presently enjoy.

The Victoria Cross

by
Sid Lindsay

Instituted on 29 January 1856, the Victoria Cross is awarded only to those of the armed forces who merit the honour – 'For Conspicuous Bravery'. The principle has been upheld that no other circumstances, neither rank, nor length of service nor severity of wounds would be considered. Initially it was awarded retrospectively to cover the Crimean War (1854-1856) and the first 62 Victoria Crosses were presented by HM Queen Victoria in Hyde Park, London on 26 June 1857.

The Cross is described as a 'cross patée of bronze, one and a half inches in diameter', and is made from the metal of Russian guns captured at Sevastopol. In the centre is the Royal Crown surmounted by a lion and beneath is a scroll with the words 'For Valour' inscribed. The date of the act of gallantry is engraved on the reverse side and the holder's name is to be found on the reverse of the clasp. The ribbon was originally blue for the Royal Navy and red for the Army, but under a Royal Warrant of 1920 this was changed to crimson for both services.

The Victoria Cross has precedence and is worn before all other decorations and on the left breast. If the ribbon only is worn, a small replica of the Cross is fixed in the centre. The award is not given lightly for there is strict scrutiny of every recommendation. A comparison seems to show that the Cross may have been awarded more frequently before the 1914-18 War than since the end of that war – for instance, the number of Victoria Crosses awarded in the Indian Mutiny was the same as for the whole of the Second World War. It must be remembered, however, that at that time the only other award available to recognise bravery in service was the Distinguished Conduct Medal, whereas now there are ten alternative honours. It would seem that a most important criterion for the Victoria Cross is that of self-sacrifice – an act of heroism, often performed on more than one occasion, in which the individual, regardless of his own safety, attempts to rescue, protect or support his fellow men or vital equipment in the face of the enemy. It also includes acts of daring leadership to secure objectives in the face of tremendous danger and in doing so to save lives and restore faltering morale. This booklet gives examples of both.

The total number of Victoria Crosses awarded up to now stands at 1355, including one to the American Unknown Soldier. 112 were awarded in the Crimean War; 182 in the Indian Mutiny; 225 for the China Campaign, Zulu War, Sudan and South African Wars. In the Great War (1914-1920), 633 were awarded; in the inter-war years, 5; and in the Second World War, 182. Since then 4 were awarded in Korea, 1 in Sarawak, 4 to Australians in Vietnam, 2 in the Falklands Conflict of 1982 and one in Iraq.

Only three people have earned double VCs; three have been awarded to fathers and sons; and four pairs of brothers have earned the award. The youngest winners – Thomas Flynn in the Indian Mutiny and Andrew Fitzgibbon in the China War of 1860 – were both just 15 years old. The oldest recipient is believed to be William Raynor during the Indian Mutiny, who was nearly 62 years of age. Accepting that the Victoria Cross is awarded only during times of conflict, it is not surprising that there are now very few surviving holders of the award. In 1952, there were 412 surviving holders; by 1976 that number had fallen to 117; and in 1984 there were only 68, of whom only 8 remained from the 1914-18 war. There are now only 12 survivors – none from the First World War – including the most recent, Private Johnson Beharry. 8 survive from the Second World War, including Merseyside's Lt Commander Ian Fraser. The last surviving Great War recipient was Air Commodore Ferdinand M.F.West who earned his VC on 10 August 1918 in France, serving with 8 Squadron Royal Air Force and died almost 80 years later in 1998. The two Falklands War recipients, Colonel H.Jones and Sergeant I.J.McKay, received their awards posthumously.

Holders of the Victoria Cross below the rank of commissioned officer were granted pensions, initially of £10 per year with £5 for a Bar. Paltry as this sum may seem, it was to remain unchanged until 1959 when the sum was increased to £100 per year, tax free, and all ranks became eligible. In 1995, the annual pension was increased to £1300. Interestingly, in a *Daily Mirror* report on 31 January 2006 about surviving VC holders, it was noted that Tulbahadur Pun VC, a Gurkha living in Nepal, was obliged to sell his VC because of financial hardship, whilst Bhanbhagta Gurung, another Gurkha also living in Nepal, found that his £1300 annual pension made him 'one of the richest men in the region'.

In the original Royal Warrant there was an expulsion clause which would permit a recipient's name to be erased from the Register for certain discreditable conduct and thereby cancel the pension. HM King George V felt strongly that there should never be any circumstances which should make the award forfeit and although the expulsion clause still remains it is highly unlikely ever to be invoked.

In 1902, King Edward VII approved the important principle of awarding the Victoria Cross posthumously; and in 1911, King George V decreed the eligibility of native officers and men of the Indian Army. In 1920, the award was extended to include the Royal Air Force and 'matrons, sisters and nurses, serving regularly or temporarily under orders, direction or supervision of the military authorities'. The decoration has never, as yet, been awarded to a woman.

One important aspect of the award is contained in what is referred to as 'Rule 13' of the Royal Warrant of 29 January 1856 :

It is ordained that, in the event of a gallant and daring act having been performed by a squadron, ship's company, a detached body of Seamen and Marines not under 50 in number, or by a brigade, regiment company or troop, in which the Admiral, General or other Officer Commanding such forces may deem that all are equally brave and distinguished so that no special selection can be made by them, then in such case the Admiral, General or Officer Commanding may direct that for any such body of Seamen or Marines, or for every troop or company of Soldiers, that one Officer shall be selected by the Officers engaged for the decoration. And in a like manner one Petty Officer or Non-commissioned Officer shall be selected by the Petty Officers and Non-commissioned Officers engaged and two Seamen or Private Soldiers or Marines shall be selected by the Seamen, Private Soldiers or Marines engaged respectively, for the decoration; and the names of those selected shall be transmitted by the Senior Officer in command of the Naval Force, Brigade, Regiment, Company or Troop, to the Admiral or General Officer Commanding who shall in due manner confer the decoration as if the acts were done under his own eye.

That paragraph takes some reading but has affected the award to a number of recipients over the years (see for example Ronald Neil Stuart VC elsewhere in this book).

In January 2006, the VC holders still surviving were:

Eric Wilson, East Surrey Regiment, August 1940 in Somaliland. Now 93 years of age.

Tulbahadur Pun, 6th Gurkha Rifles, June 1944 in Burma. Now 82 years of age.

John Cruickshank, Royal Air Force Volunteer Reserve, July 1944 over the Atlantic. Now 85 years of age.

Tasker Watkins, The Welsh Regiment, August 1944 in Normandy. Now 87 years of age.

Bhanbhagta Gurung, 2nd Gurkha Rifles, March 1945 in Burma. Now 85 years of age.

Lachhiman Gurung, 8th Gurkha Rifles, May 1945 in Burma. Now 87 years of age.

Ted Kenna, Australian Imperial Force, May 1945 in New Guinea. Now aged 86 years.

Ian Fraser, Royal Naval Reserve, May 1945 in Singapore Harbour. Now 85 years of age.

Bill Speakman, Black Watch, November 1951 in Korea. Now 77 years of age.

Rambahadur Limbu, 2nd Battalion, 10th Princess Mary's Own Gurkha Rifles, November 1965 in Borneo. Now 66 years old.

Keith Payne, 1st Battalion Royal Australian Regiment, May 1969, in Vietnam. Now 72 years old.

Johnson Beharry, Princess of Wales's Royal Regiment, May 2004 in Iraq. Now 26 years old.

The Memorial

The Memorial to Noel Chavasse, VC and Bar, an adopted son of Liverpool, and 15 other recipients of the Victoria Cross who were born in Liverpool, is the brainchild of local Chavasse admirers. They met in July 2005 and declared their intention of securing a fitting memorial. Ambitious? Optimistic? Foolhardy? My answer to each would have to be 'Yes!' – but the group's determination to succeed has never wavered.

The sculptor is a local man, Tom Murphy, who has a long history of producing memorable pieces in Liverpool. He is responsible for the Shankly statue at Liverpool Football Club, the John Lennon statue at our airport, the Moores Brothers statue formerly in Church Street but now in Old Hall Street, the Captain Johnny Walker statue at the Pier Head, the Blitz Memorial at Liverpool Parish Church, and many others. It seemed logical to us that Tom should be our man, especially as we knew he shared our admiration for Chavasse and our other 'Liverpool Heroes'. We consulted the Chavasse family and the Regimental Associations and all agreed that we should aim for a traditional bronze work which would strive to show the character and personality of Noel Chavasse, rather than a particular

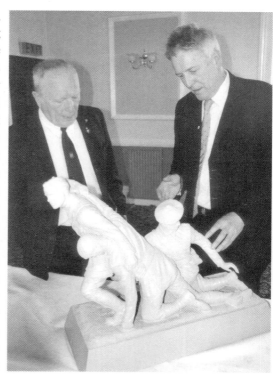

Bill Sergeant (left, Chairman of NCVCMA) and Tom Murphy (sculptor) with the model of the VC Memorial (November 2005).
Courtesy Roy Bevan

moment in history. We also agreed that both the Royal Army Medical Corps and the Liverpool Scottish allegiances of Chavasse should feature, together with one of his stretcher-bearers - Noel was always anxious to remind people of their bravery. Within these parameters, Tom's design has found favour not only with us but also with the family and military, and I leave it to him to describe our memorial.

Bill Sergeant, Chairman, NCVCMA

Design of the NCVCMA Memorial

It was decided almost from the outset that the Chavasse sculpture celebrating the heroic deeds of Captain Noel Chavasse could not be depicted using a single figure. He was not a glory seeker; his deeds arose from his dedication as a doctor, a real professional and above all a committed Christian. He would not have been comfortable with a statue which did not pay tribute to a brave stretcher-bearer. A wounded soldier became the third figure.

A three-figure grouping provided an ideal opportunity for an action sculpture, and a work which is meant to be interesting from all viewing angles. The sculptural group forms an offset triangle, or a wave set on a slight gradient. The angular lines throughout the piece create an impression of forward propulsion and a sense of struggle. In line with the conditions of the time, the figures look as if they are on an endless challenging journey.

The figures are displayed on an oblong base reminiscent of the Cenotaph, and the sloped sides of the base include tributes to 15 Liverpool-born Victoria Cross winners. Captain Chavasse is portrayed straining under the weight of the wounded soldier, whose whole body and arms are extended across the length of the sculpture in a cruciform shape.

The sculpture has many fine details: Chavasse himself is depicted wearing the Liverpool Scottish Glengarry with his RAMC uniform – perhaps not strictly accurate in the context of battle but symbolic of his everlasting affection for the Liverpool Battalion. He supports a wounded soldier by stretching his right arm over his shoulder and clasping the wrist of the wounded man. At the same time, he supports the wounded man's upper torso with his other arm. The powerful stretcher-bearer at the rear contorts his body to assist in the lift, and his concern for the wounded man's obvious ankle injury is apparent. In this kneeling position, the famous Liverpool Scottish kilt is clearly displayed. The close contact of the figures, which almost seem to be welded together, echoes the compassion and camaraderie of soldiers.

The design sets out to maintain the viewer's interest throughout with the dramatic positions of the figures set at differing heights, and the mass of detail, including the way the hands are depicted - some coupled together and others stretched out dramatically - and the detail of the badges and uniforms of the RAMC, the King's Liverpool Regiment and the Liverpool Scottish.

I have deliberately omitted any reference to the weapons of war as this sculpture is primarily about the triumph of love and compassion in laying down one's life for another. This message will be as relevant for generations to come as it was in 1914-18. It is important to emphasise that although this memorial depicts Noel Chavasse, it nevertheless commemorates the valour and deeds of fifteen other recipients of the Victoria Cross, several of whom, like Chavasse, lost their lives whilst helping their fellow men. Chavasse epitomises the bravery of all such men to whom this memorial is a lasting tribute.

I am proud to have been chosen for this Commission. My words do it scant justice for, after all, this sculpture is meant to be seen.

Tom Murphy, Sculptor

Noel Godfrey Chavasse
VC & BAR, MC

by
Ann Clayton
(Author of Chavasse: Double VC, Pen & Sword Books 1992)

Noel Godfrey Chavasse was born on 9 November 1884 at 36 New Inn Hall Street, Oxford. He and his twin brother Christopher Maude were the sons of the Rev. Francis James Chavasse, Rector of St Peter-le-Bailey, Oxford, and Edith Chavasse (née Maude) daughter of the Rev Joseph Maude, Vicar of Chirk in Denbighshire. The Chavasse family were of French origin, and had arrived in England in the eighteenth century, settling in the Oxfordshire and Birmingham areas. Francis and Edith Chavasse already had a daughter, Dorothea, and later had twin daughters, Marjorie and May, and two further sons, Bernard and Aidan.

Capt. N.G. Chavasse VC & BAR, MC, February 1917

Noel and Christopher were educated first at Magdalen College School, Oxford, but in 1900 their father was appointed Bishop of Liverpool, and the family moved to the city which was home to Noel for the rest of his life. They lived in the Bishop's Palace at 19 Abercromby Square. Bishop Chavasse soon began the biggest project of his life - the construction of a cathedral. All of the Chavasse boys were educated at Liverpool College, then situated in Sefton Park Road, Toxteth, and Noel and Christopher excelled at rugby, running and cricket, as well as acquitting themselves well in academic subjects. In 1904 they went up to Trinity College, Oxford, where Noel graduated in 1908 with first-class honours. While at Oxford both he and his brother were awarded their Blues for running, and represented Great Britain in the 400 metres event at the London Olympic Games in 1908, though not winning any medals. Noel subsequently read medicine at Liverpool University, qualifying as a doctor in 1912. He took up a post at the Liverpool Royal Southern Hospital under the renowned orthopaedic consultant, Robert Jones – this experience was of enormous value to Noel during the Great War, when he was faced with innumerable difficult surgical problems in caring for the men of his battalion. Christopher was ordained by his father and held a curacy in St Helens.

**N.G. Chavasse medal group,
Imperial War Museum**

While at Oxford Noel had joined the University Officer Training Corps, and back in Liverpool, in 1913, he joined the RAMC (Territorial Force); he was soon attached to the 10th Bn the King's (Liverpool) Regiment – the Liverpool Scottish. He also spent much of his leisure time helping underprivileged lads in deprived areas of Liverpool, demonstrating a lifelong concern for those in need.

At the outbreak of war on 4 August 1914, Noel Chavasse was in camp with the Liverpool Scottish near Lancaster, but they were quickly recalled to Liverpool and were mobilised – one of the earliest territorial battalions to be sent to France. Noel wrote to his parents, on the eve of his departure to the war:

> *Goodbye, my dear Father. I am going to do my best to be a faithful soldier of Jesus Christ and St George. Your loving son Noel.*

He had an unquestioning patriotism and an unshakeable belief that God was on the side of England.

The battalion arrived at the front on 2 November, and were soon involved in the often atrocious battle conditions of what became known as the First Battle of Ypres. Noel's efforts for the welfare of his men soon became legendary. He trained his stretcher-bearers in first aid, improved on the standard-issue stretcher and devised a better method for the splinting of fractures, as well as a more effective model for a trench hospital. He organised the provision of numerous extra comforts for the troops, and performed some remarkable feats of surgery in appalling conditions. His letters home showed that he cared deeply about the harsh conditions endured by his men, as this one shows:

> *Our men have had a terrible experience of 72 hours in trenches, drenched through and in some places knee-deep in mud and water. To see them come out, and line up, and march off is almost terrible. They don't look like strong young men. They are muddied to the eyes. Their coats are plastered with mud and weigh an awful weight with the water which has soaked in. Their backs are bent, and they stagger and totter along with the weight of their packs. Their faces are white and haggard and their eyes glare out from mud which with short, bristly beards gives them an almost beastlike look. They look like wounded or sick wild things. I have seen nothing like it.... Many, too many, who are quite beat, have to be told they must walk it. Then comes a nightmare of a march for about 2 to 4 miles, when the men walk in a trance...*

His generous sympathy towards his fellow-man applied to all – he expressed care and understanding towards German people, and empathised with men whose nerve had gone, at times helping them to cover up their self-inflicted wounds and earning himself rebukes in the process.

The Chavasse family at 19 Abercromby Square, Liverpool, c. 1912. Seated, Left to right: Dorothea, The Bishop, Mrs Chavasse, Rev. Foster-Carter. Standing, left to right: Bernard, Marjorie, Christopher, Noel, May, Aidan.

Courtesy Chavasse family

The other Chavasse children were playing their parts in the war too. Christopher, Noel's twin brother, was serving as an army chaplain, while younger brother Bernard was Medical Officer to the 17th Bn the King's (Liverpool) Regiment – one of the Liverpool Pals battalions. In the same battalion was youngest brother Aidan, a second lieutenant. Noel's elder sister

Dorothea, married by now and with a young family, nevertheless busied herself with providing support for her brother – he once asked for new socks for the whole battalion, and within days she had organised friends into providing 1000 pairs. Marjorie stayed at home to assist her parents, especially the Bishop whose motor-car she drove with spirit. May served for almost the whole of the war as a 'ward maid' in the Liverpool Merchant's Mobile Hospital at Etaples.

On 16 June 1915, near the village of Hooge along the Menin Road near Ypres, the Liverpool Scottish were part of an assault on the German front line. The losses for the battalion were such that it practically ceased to exist – 23 officers and 519 Other Ranks went into the battle, but only two officers and 140 men came through unscathed. Many of the dead were friends of Noel's from peacetime days, and most have no known grave but are commemorated on the Menin Gate in Ypres. Much selfless bravery was displayed that day, and a large list of names was put forward for awards. Noel was awarded the Military Cross, for his 'inspiring example... to his untiring efforts in personally searching the ground between our line and the enemy's many of the wounded owe their lives'. The Military Cross was presented to him by HM King George V at Buckingham Palace on 7 June 1916. In March 1916 Noel had become engaged to his cousin, Gladys Chavasse. She was the daughter of the Bishop's late brother, Sir Thomas Chavasse, who had been a prominent surgeon in Birmingham, although the family lived in Bromsgrove.

In the Battle of the Somme which began on 1 July 1916, the Liverpool Scottish, now part of the 55th (West Lancashire) Division, were given an objective as difficult as that at Hooge. They were to attack the village of Guillemont. Their advance began on the night of 8/9 August, under murderous conditions, again with many casualties. Once again, the 'Doc' demonstrated the greatest of courage, and a total lack of concern for his own safety. He was awarded the Victoria Cross, and the *London Gazette* citation dated 26 October 1916 tells its own story:

> *During an attack he tended the wounded in the open all day, under heavy fire, frequently in view of the enemy. During the ensuing night he searched for wounded on the ground in front of the enemy's lines for four hours. Next day he took one stretcher-bearer to the advanced trenches, and, under heavy fire, carried an urgent case for 500 yards into safety, being wounded in the side by a splinter during the journey. The same night he took up a party of trusty volunteers, rescued three*

wounded men from a shell-hole twenty-five yards from the enemy's trench, buried the bodies of two officers, and collected many identity discs, although fired on by bombs and machine guns. Altogether he saved the lives of some twenty badly wounded men, besides the ordinary cases which passed through his hands. His courage and self-sacrifice were beyond praise.

The city of Liverpool received the news with great satisfaction, and the Bishop and other members of the family were congratulated wherever they went. Noel received large numbers of letters, which he endeavoured to answer in his billet; his modest reply to one of them demonstrated his quiet acceptance of what he felt was simply his duty:

It is a real pleasure to be able to do anything for our soldiers, and I do count myself very fortunate to be able, by reason of age and good health, to serve them out here. ...And certainly our soldiers do deserve all we can do for them. Every day I admire and love them more for their courage and cheery endurance...

The Victoria Cross was presented to Noel by HM King George V, again at Buckingham Palace, on 5 February 1917. The last studio photograph of him was taken soon afterwards. Then it was back to the front, and later that year, in the Battle of Passchendaele, Noel Chavasse lost his life while again saving others.

This battle, known also as the Third Battle of Ypres, resulted from the decision of the British High Command to take the offensive in the Ypres Salient and northwards to the coast, in order to force the enemy to retreat. During a preliminary reconnaissance along the Menin Road, Noel's youngest brother Aidan was missing, believed killed. His body was never found, and his name appears on the Menin Gate. Noel knew about this sad event, and like all the family was deeply distressed by it.

But he had to concentrate on the battle to come. It began on 31 July 1917; at the height of summer when fair weather might be expected, and Sir Douglas Haig expected good progress to be made. The 55th (West Lancashire) Division, of which the Liverpool Scottish were a part, had as its objective the German-held area in the vicinity of Wieltje, and at 3.30 am on 31 July they were already in open ground and moving forwards. Heavy machine-gun fire held the Liverpool men up as did a mass of uncut barbed wire, but they pressed on. Early in the assault Noel was hit in the head by a shell splinter, but he refused to go back for treatment. Within hours all the early objectives were taken. The Liverpool Scottish established an HQ in a farmhouse, and Noel set up his regimental aid post nearby in an abandoned German dugout.

Officers of the Liverpool Scottish at Tonbridge Wells, October 1914.
Noel Chavasse RAMC, centre back.

At about 8 o'clock in the evening it began to rain – an unending, teeming downpour so typical of Flanders. The ground turned to mud, shell-holes filled up, and moving anywhere at all proved almost impossible. Noel was again wounded on 1 August but still refused treatment. Finally, on 2 August, while he was sitting on a chair in the aid post trying to get some rest, a shell from the direction of the retreating German troops entered through the doorway of the dugout and exploded, killing or wounding everyone inside. Noel was mortally wounded. It was an abdominal wound, which he knew was serious, but he still managed to drag himself out to look for help for the others injured in the dugout – most, however, were already dead. He was picked up by a RAMC Ambulance and conveyed back to a light railway line which had been set up for the purpose. From here he was taken to Brandhoek, a few miles behind the lines.

Here he was first seen at 46th Field Ambulance, commanded by Lt Col Arthur Martin-Leake, who was the first man ever to have been awarded a second Victoria Cross – a Bar to his VC gained in the Boer War in 1902. Martin-Leake realised he could do nothing for the terrible wound, and ordered that Noel be rushed to the nearby No. 32 Casualty Clearing Station which had specialist doctors. They operated, but Noel Chavasse died on 4 August 1917 at 1pm. One of the last things he did was to ask for a message to be conveyed to Gladys, his fiancée:

> *Please tell her, duty called, and called me to obey.*

He was buried in the Brandhoek New Military Cemetery – nearby in the same cemetery is the grave of Charles Arundel Rudd, his batman, who was mortally wounded in the same incident.

The news reached Liverpool a few days later, and messages of sympathy began to flood into the Bishop's Palace, including one from the King. Then, in September, the Bishop received a letter from Lord Derby, informing him that it had been decided to award Noel a Bar to his Victoria Cross. The Bishop wrote to his son Bernard:

> *(He) literally laid down his life for his men... he was indeed a hero, and... he was a man of valour because he was a man of God. Continually your dear Mother and I thank and glorify God for such a son and for his wonderful and beautiful life spent in helping others, and crowned at last by his noble death...*

The citation for Noel's second VC, in the *London Gazette* on 14 September, read as follows:

> *Though severely wounded early in the action whilst carrying a wounded soldier to the dressing station he refused to leave his post, and for two days not only continued to perform his duties but in addition went out repeatedly under heavy fire to search for and attend to the wounded who were lying out. During these searches, although practically without food during this period, worn with fatigue and faint with his wound, he assisted to carry in a number of badly wounded men over heavy and difficult ground. By his extraordinary energy and inspiring example he was instrumental in rescuing many wounded who would have otherwise undoubtedly succumbed under the bad weather conditions. This devoted and gallant officer subsequently died of his wounds.*

The Bar was presented to the Bishop privately by a senior Army officer later in the year. Noels' twin brother Christopher, and his younger surviving brother

Bernard, were each also awarded Military Crosses that summer. May was Mentioned in Despatches for her work at the Liverpool Merchants Mobile Hospital.

Postscript

Bishop Chavasse retired to Oxford in 1923 (the first part of 'his' cathedral was consecrated in 1924), and died in 1928, a year after his beloved wife Edith. Christopher Chavasse married and had four children; he founded St Peter's College Oxford in memory of his father, and went on to achieve high office in the Church of England, ultimately becoming Bishop of Rochester, and died in 1962. Bernard Chavasse also married, and had three children; he became a well-known eye surgeon in Liverpool, and died in 1941. Unlike their older sister Dorothea, neither May nor Marjorie married, but they did live to see their 100th birthday, and were the excited recipients of telegrams from the Queen to celebrate the rather unusual occasion of twin centenarians. Marjorie died in 1987, and May died in 1989. Gladys Chavasse married an army chaplain and spent a number of years overseas; they had no children, and she died in 1962.

Only three men have ever been awarded the Victoria Cross twice:

- **Lt Col Arthur Martin-Leake**, RAMC, 1902 (South Africa) and 1914 (France & Flanders), died 1953;

- **Captain Noel G. Chavasse**, RAMC, 1916 and 1917 (both France & Flanders), died of wounds 1917;

- **Captain Charles Hazlitt Upham**, New Zealand Infantry (Canterbury Regiment), 1941 (Crete) and 1942 (Western Desert), died 1994.

The three men are connected: Chavasse was examined by Martin-Leake on being brought out of the trenches mortally wounded; and the Upham and Chavasse families were distantly related (by marriage).

Noel Chavasse's medals were held by St Peter's College, Oxford, until recent years. In February 1990 they were presented to the Imperial War Museum, London, on permanent loan, at a ceremony held in the presence of HM Queen Elizabeth the Queen Mother. They may be seen, together with other Chavasse family awards, in the Victoria Cross gallery.

There are (or were) memorial tablets and inscriptions to Captain Noel Chavasse in the following locations, but nowhere is there yet a sculpted memorial:

Magdalen College School, Oxford;

Liverpool College;

House of Lords;

St Peter's College Chapel, Oxford;

Library of Trinity College, Oxford;

Royal Southern Hospital, Liverpool (tablet now missing, and the hospital has been demolished);

Liverpool University;

Liverpool Medical Institution;

Liverpool Cathedral Diocesan Book of Remembrance;

Liverpool Town Hall, Hall of Remembrance;

208 Hospital, TA/RAMC, Chavasse House, Childwall;

Liverpool Scottish Museum;

Liverpool Cricket Club;

Wavertree RBL;

Chavasse Court, Lord Street, Liverpool (recently demolished);

Brandhoek Church entrance, Belgium;

An 'English Heritage' Blue Plaque at 19 Abercromby Square, Liverpool;

Chavasse Park, Liverpool, currently being developed by Grosvenor Estates, where a memorial is planned;

Noel Chavasse VC Memorial Association; proposed memorial sculpture as described in this book.

Grave of Capt. N.G. Chavasse at Brandhoek, Belgium.

His father, the Bishop of Liverpool, chose the inscription.

It is the only Commonwealth War Graves Commission headstone to carry two representations of the Victoria Cross.

English Heritage Blue Plaque at 19 Abercromby Square, Liverpool.

John Kirk VC

A s is the case with several of the earliest recipients of the Victoria Cross, little is known of Kirk's early life. He is believed to have been born in Liverpool in July 1827, although even this date is at variance with his declared age when he died. It is said that he was either born in the Liverpool Workhouse on Brownlow Hill, or entered it at a very young age. Nothing is known of his parents, and one source suggests that the name John Kirk was given to him by those who found him. It seems very likely that his early life was one of poverty and as was not unusual he saw Army life as a way to survive. He is known to have enlisted in the 10th Regiment (later to become the Lincolnshire Regiment) and was posted to the 7th Company. (The recently published 1841 Census shows only one John Kirk living in Liverpool - born about 1828, he lived at 24 Ormond Street with Elliotte Kirk, born 1801, George Kirk, born 1831 and William Kirk, born 1791. It is possible that this is our man.)

Records suggest that he was not a particularly good soldier and was frequently in trouble as a result of drunkenness, but when sober he performed as well as the rest of his Company and certainly did nothing so seriously wrong as to merit discharge. He spent most of his service in India, taking part in the Punjab campaign of 1848-49 and held the Campaign Medal with two bars for action at Mooltan and Goojerrat. It was during the Indian Mutiny that he was to write his name in history, however.

The part played by the 10th Regiment in the suppression of the Mutiny began on 22 May 1857, when news came of an outbreak at the city of Benares, where the 13th Irregular Cavalry, a regiment of Sikhs, was stationed together with the 37th Native Cavalry. It had been decided to disarm the 37th, for signs of discontent were such that all of the horrors of the Mutiny were certain to follow unless assistance came. At once, Captains Norman and Annesley, with Ensign Donald and 167 men, were sent from Dinapore to Benares to protect the garrison from the mutineers. When they arrived and the disarming of the 37th began, there ensued a fight which saw two men of the 10th killed and eight mortally wounded.

It was during this fight that 2359 Pte John Kirk earned his Victoria Cross for an act of bravery on 4 June. The troops of the 10th were engaged rescuing any Europeans who were still out in the lines and who might well be cut off, when Kirk heard that Captain Brown, the Pension Paymaster, and his wife and small child, with their servants and others who had sought safety in the Captain's bungalow, were now surrounded by the rebels and in grave danger. Kirk immediately went to the scene, meeting up with Sergeant Majors Peter Gill and Matthew Rosamund, who had volunteered to try to save Captain Brown and his party. When they arrived, the bungalow was being fired on but they rushed to the building, without being hit, and began firing back at the attackers, with such effect that they forced the rebels to withdraw. They led the frightened party from the bungalow to the safety of the garrison, always with the possibility that they would again be attacked on the way. The manner in which they carried out this rescue was deemed to merit the highest bravery award.

So it was that three years later, on 9 November 1860, Pte John Kirk went to Home Park, Windsor, to be presented with his Cross by Queen Victoria. He was accompanied by Pte Dennis Dempsey of the same Regiment, who had also earned a VC. Her Majesty was totally unaware that just two days before his heroic act, John Kirk had been given 50 lashes for misbehaviour, being 'drunk on the march'. He had taken his punishment without too much rancour, which says much for his stalwart character when sober. He was said to have a fine singing voice, often apparent while marching, no doubt to the delight of his fellow-soldiers but not always in tune with his superior officers, who knew that his singing was usually the result of over-imbibing! He was never without his 'bladder of arrack' when on the march: this was a small skin pouch hung around his neck on a cord and concealed beneath his tunic. This pouch was known by the men as a 'bishop', while 'arrack' was a distilled spirit of rice or coconut palm of dubious purity but commonplace in India and Burma.

Poor John Kirk - despite his courage and the honour he had earned for himself, his regiment and his home town, he lacked the moral fibre to be an upright, decent man. He was an illiterate 'loser', an habitual drunkard frequently punished for his many indiscretions, whose Army Medical record showed him 'no longer fit to discharge his duties of a soldier' due to his having contracted 'Chronic Syphilitic Rheumatism'. Syphilis, 'which occurred in the service but not by the service' was given as the primary cause of Kirk's incapacity, and was 'aggravated by the use of intoxicating liquors or indulgence in other habits or vices'. He was discharged on medical grounds (and not 'dismissed' from the service) while the regiment was in Ireland in May 1864 – he 'made his mark' on the discharge papers as he could not sign his name.

He worked for some time as a labourer in Liverpool, as far as is known never marrying, and eventually died in the Liverpool Workhouse, Brownlow Hill, on 31 August 1865, aged 40. The cause of death was shown as 'Phthisis', almost certainly pulmonary tuberculosis. I have heard it said recently that John Kirk might have suffered from a form of narcolepsy, which causes drowsiness and could well have been the cause of his problems rather than drunkenness. There is something noble about the bravery of an otherwise problematic soldier. How often have we been entertained in war films by the behaviour of the recalcitrant, awkward soldier who, when the crunch comes, is portrayed as showing hitherto unsuspected bravery? The definition of bravery is often debated but remains indefinable – what is a matter of routine for one man may demand immeasurable nerve from another. Similarly, that vital spark within a man which leads him to perform the kind of deeds which Kirk and our other 'Liverpool Heroes' did, seems to be alive within the soul of so many different characters. One could be forgiven for expecting displays of courage, self-discipline and indeed self-sacrifice from those brought up against a military background, or even those with a certain educational, religious or 'cultured' background as exemplified by those Army padres who earned the Victoria Cross; or deeply religious men who gave their all for their fellows, such as Noel Chavasse and others. It is not really surprising to learn that Eton former pupils were awarded more VCs than any other body of men. Yet the deeds of David Jones, Albert White, William Ratcliffe and John Kirk show that education, status in life, religious or family background do not of themselves make a man a hero, any more than their absence precludes bravery.

Postscript

For many years, nothing was known of the burial place of this tragic man, who came into the world unknown and unloved and died 40 years later, still unknown and probably unwanted. The 1861 Census shows a John Kirk, 34 years of age, born in Liverpool, occupation farm servant, living in barracks at Aldershot with the rank of private. However, careful research by Maurice Rigby has traced his burial place to Anfield Cemetery, Liverpool. Cemetery records confirm that he was buried in Grave 2318 on 3 September 1865, his last address being 'Work House' and his profession shown as 'Soldier'. The record also shows that his burial cost the City just 12/6d (62.5p), including the fees of the clerk and vicar. As a result of the efforts of Maurice, on 5 June 1989, almost exactly 132 years after Kirk won his VC, a service of dedication was held at the cemetery for the erection of a headstone in his memory: he was the very first Liverpool man to earn the honour, and had lain in a common grave since 1865. Maurice made representations to Liverpool City Council and to the Royal Anglian Regiment (now incorporating the Lincolnshire Regiment) and the outcome was a magnificent headstone of black Indian granite, with inscribed gold lettering and an engraved Victoria Cross - a fitting tribute to this simple but courageous soldier. The ceremony was conducted by the Reverend John Duffield, curate of the local church, and was attended by Major General Sir Welby-Everard and Major General Gerard Wright, both trustees of the Anglian Regiment; Mrs Dorothy Gavin, Chairman of the City Council, with other members of the City Council; members of the Royal British Legion; and Joe Lynch GC BEM represented the Victoria Cross and George Cross Association. Also present were the stonemasons whose beautifully carved work is now on permanent display. This is a worthy monument made even more poignant by the magnificent gesture by the Council of including on the base of the stone the names of the other five poor souls buried in the same paupers' grave (above).

John Kirk's VC was bought by Lieut Col E.P.Lloyd, CBE DSO, who presented it to the 2nd Bn, Royal Lincolnshire Regiment (now, through amalgamations, the 2nd Battalion, Royal Anglian Regiment). With Kirk's campaign medals, it is now on display in the Museum of Lincolnshire Life, Lincoln.

$\mathcal{A}$lfred Stowell Jones VC

Born on 24 January 1832, at 3 Huskisson Street, Liverpool 8, Alfred Stowell Jones was the son of Archdeacon John Jones and his wife, Hannah (daughter of John Pares, of Hopwell Hall, Derbyshire and founder of Pares Bank in Leicester). His father was the vicar of St Andrew's Episcopal Church in Renshaw Street, Liverpool and later of Christ Church, Waterloo. When the Archdeacon died in 1899 at the age of 98 he was, not surprisingly, the oldest Merseyside preacher.

Alfred was educated at Liverpool College, Shaw Street, Liverpool and from there went to the Royal Military Academy at Sandhurst. He joined the 9th Lancers on a paid commission as a Cornet (a junior commissioned officer of a Cavalry Troop who carried the standard) and on 21 September 1855 was appointed lieutenant and posted to India with his regiment. It was here, in the course of the well-documented Indian Mutiny, that he was to earn his nation's highest decoration for bravery.

On 8 June 1857, at Budli-ka-Serai, Lt Jones, leading the right troop of the 4th Squadron of the 9th Lancers, galloped to investigate a cloud of dust in the distance, believed to have been caused by enemy guns on the move. Looking to the left flank of his squadron, he saw a nine-pounder gun drawn by six horses with drivers, moving away from the dust cloud as if to create a diversion. Leaving the 4th Squadron to pursue the main enemy force, Jones turned his Arab charger and, when clear of the ranks, raced after the escaping enemy gun. The six mutineer drivers, looking over their shoulders, saw him on their trail and began flogging their horses in an attempt to outpace him. Very soon, however, Jones was alongside the off-wheeler and with his sword cut down the driver, who fell between the wheel horses. Jones grabbed the bridle and was able to bring the whole team to a standstill. At this point, he was joined by Regimental Sergeant Thonger and three troopers and together they attacked the drivers of the lead horses causing them to fall under the feet of their horses, killing them instantly. Cavalry Officers had been issued with steel spikes as a precaution. Where abandoned artillery was likely to fall into the hands of mutineers, the spikes were to be used to render the guns useless by driving the steel spike into the vent hole on the cannon, which Jones duly did. The 4th Squadron, unable to overtake the dust-cloud, rejoined the Regimental Troop Leader, together with three other Squadrons under Col Yule, 9th Lancers. Col Yule, seeing ammunition in the gun limber, caused the gun to be reactivated and fired a few rounds at a nearby fortified village occupied by mutineers, after which Jones was permitted to seize his prize. Seeing that the four lead-horses had been injured by their falling drivers, he borrowed a pair of horses from the Artillery and used these as the wheel horses with his own men as drivers. They then took the gun to their camp being established under the ridge at Delhi. The gun had in fact belonged to Captain de Tessier's Field Battery, which had mutinied at Delhi the month before and had been actively used by the rebels. It was now handed back to the Artillery.

Col Hope Grant reported the incident as a 'well-thought-out plan, gallantly executed', and it earned Alfred Stowell Jones his VC.

In a matter of weeks, on 10 October 1857, Jones was again involved in recapturing a gun from the enemy, this incident almost costing him his life. He was with Captain French, leading their Squadron of 9th Lancers, when they met a much larger force of enemy cavalry. In the ensuing battle, Captain French was killed, while Jones was struck by a musket ball through his bridle arm, causing him to fall from his horse. While on the ground, Lt Jones was slashed by a sabre more than 20 times and left for dead. The squadron routed the rebels, recovering a valuable gun which had earlier been stolen from the Artillery, and returned to find Jones alive but suffering from severe loss of blood. He was immediately taken to receive medical aid and survived. For his services in the Mutiny Campaign, Jones received the Mutiny Medal with two clasps, was promoted to Captain and Brevet Major and was also Mentioned in Despatches on three occasions. On hearing of his VC award, Jones commented that if he had been riding a slower horse, and if he had been unable to capture the gun, he would probably have been court-martialled for breaking the ranks during an operation. With 11 other recipients, Jones was presented with his Victoria Cross by Queen

Victoria on Southsea Common. Ironically, at the Cavalry School, Leeds, a few days earlier, Jones had been breaking in some young horses when one of them threw its head suddenly, catching him a nasty blow on his eyebrow, and so he appeared before Her Majesty with a badly bruised face.

His army career continued and Jones was appointed DAQMG to the Cavalry with the Delhi Field Force. In this capacity, he devoted much of his time to the problems of hygiene and sanitation which constantly troubled military establishments. In 1860, he became a major and graduated at the Staff College.

In 1863, Jones married Emily, the youngest daughter of John Back of Surrey, and together they had five sons and a daughter. One son, a lieutenant in the 11th Hussars, was killed in India in a polo accident in 1895. The following year, a second son, Lt Tertius Jones of the Royal Horse Artillery, died at Meerut, India. In 1914, his eldest son, Captain Owen Jones, RN, commander of the battleship Africa, died of Bright's Disease. The fourth son, Captain Harry Jones, an indigo planter at Tirhoot, India, was killed in action with the 13th Lancers in the battle for Samara, Mesopotamia, on 2 November 1917. Another son, Captain Owen Jones, Royal Naval Reserve, became an Elder Brother of Trinity House. Jones' daughter married Major, later Major-General, W.A.Watson, son of General Sir John Watson, GCMG.

As Lieutenant Colonel, Alfred Jones VC was appointed manager of all sewage works of the 1st Army Corps in Aldershot Command and held this position from 1895 until 1912, when he retired from the Service. In 1878 he was appointed a Member of the Institute of Civil Engineers and was later a founder member of the Royal Sanitary Institute. He was the author of several works and technical papers on sewage treatment and communal sanitation. His wife, Emily, died in 1918 and Alfred himself died on 29 May 1920 aged 88 years, at his home in Finchampstead, Berkshire; he is buried in St James' Churchyard in Finchampstead. According to records, his medals are not on public display.

*W*illiam Connolly VC

W illiam Connolly was born in Liverpool, in 1817, possibly in May, but little is known about his early life or his parentage. We do know that he enlisted in the Army in Liverpool on 2 May, 1837, aged 20 years.

Like John Kirk and Alfred Stowell Jones, it was in the Indian Mutiny that William Connolly was to display the incredible courage which was so rightly to earn him the highest military honour for gallantry. Analysis of the causes of the Mutiny and the steps taken to quell it are well documented elsewhere and records include many instances of bravery under extreme conditions. It is generally accepted, however, that the manner in which many of the military operations were carried out by the British commanders left a great deal to be desired in terms of professional strategy. That the mutiny ever occurred at all, it has been claimed, stemmed more from the apathetic attitude of the military authorities rather than from any single act of religious offence relating to the use of animal fat in the servicing of ammunition which, some experts claim, sparked the uprising.

There had been increasing signs of unrest in the Punjab, the most threatening being uprisings at Jhelum and Sialkot. It had been known for some time that the 14th Sipahi Regiment, stationed in a cantonment on the banks of the Chenab River (now in Pakistan), was on the verge of mutiny. Sir John Lawrence dispatched a small force of guns and troops to the area with the intention of taking the Sipahi by surprise and disarming them. This force comprised some companies of the 24th Queens Regiment, guns from the Bengal Horse Artillery under Lt Henry Cooke and a party of Lind's Multani Horse, all coming under the command of Colonel Ellice of the 24th Queens. For some reason, the force commander decided not to accept the strategy which had been carefully worked out for him to gain the maximum surprise, preferring to implement his own plan of attack. The original plan had been to attack the Sipahi's unprotected rear, but Ellice decided on a direct frontal attack which had no element of surprise for the enemy. The latter were in fact on morning parade, saw the British approaching and, realising their intentions, immediately broke ranks and took up their defensive positions in the battlemented building erected by Sir Charles Napier as a defensive stronghold some years earlier. This provided the rebels with excellent protection to their front, and the mud huts in their lines had all been loopholed for additional defence in case of attack. The British force's direct assault, enthusiastic and brave though it was, was met by concentrated fire from the rebels' muskets. Lind's cavalry charged gallantly, suffering severe casualties as a result, while Cooke's artillery opened fire but from too short a range and they too were caught by the murderous enemy musketry. Despite these setbacks, the men of the Queens attacked and took the defensive guard building and as the Sipahis fell back to their lines, a well-directed shell burst amongst them, causing them to flee to the village.

The British force was by now exhausted. They had been on the march since the night before and it was now the full heat of noon. Col Ellice had been carried from the fray badly wounded and Captain Spring had been shot dead. Many men and horses had been lost – a truly Pyrrhic victory. Col Gerrard took command and instead of allowing his men sufficient time to recover, decided to pursue the Sipahis into the village. Once more the British found themselves fighting an enemy which was well protected. The artillery was brought up once more to try to force the rebels out but again the range was too short and the rebels put the gunners under severe attack. The exhausted British troops were in no state to engage in street fighting against the wily rebels and it was not long before Retreat was sounded and the British withdrew. Two guns were saved but a third, in spite of gallant efforts to recover it, was lost to the enemy, who were to use it against the retreating British.

That night the troops rested before renewing their attack on the next day; but in the morning it was found that the rebels had fled. They were caught later as they tried to find refuge and very few escaped.

In the opening attack Gunner William Connolly was to display the splendid courage described by Lt Cooke, Bengal Horse Artillery, thus :

> *About daybreak I advanced my half-troop at a gallop and engaged the enemy within easy musket range. The sponge man of one of my guns, Gunner Connolly, assumed the duties of second sponge man and had barely assisted in the discharge of his gun when a musket ball through the left thigh felled him to the ground; nothing daunted by the pain and loss of blood, he was endeavouring to regain his post when I ordered a movement in retirement and, though severely wounded, he was mounted*

on his horse in the gun team and rode to the next position which the guns took up, manfully declining to go to the rear when the necessity of him doing so was represented to him. About 11am, when the guns were still in action, the same gunner, whilst sponging, was knocked down by a musket ball striking him on the hip, thereby causing great faintness and partial unconsciousness, for the pain appeared excessive and the blood was flowing fast. On seeing this, I gave instructions for his removal from the action but this brave man, on hearing me, staggered to his feet and said 'No, Sir, I'll not go whilst I can work as sponge man'. Late in the afternoon, my three guns were engaged at 100 yards from the walls of a village, viz. the 14th Native Infantry mutineers. Amidst a storm of bullets which did great execution, Gunner Connolly, though suffering severely from his two previous wounds, was wielding his sponge with an energy and courage which attracted the admiration of his comrades and while he was cheerfully encouraging a wounded man to hasten in bringing up the ammunition, a musket ball tore through the muscles of his left leg; but with the most undaunted bravery he struggled on and not till he had loaded six times did this man give way, when through loss of blood he fell into my arms and I placed him on a wagon, which shortly afterwards bore him in a state of unconsciousness from the fight.

Although this action was on 7 July 1857, Connolly's VC was not gazetted until 3 September 1858 and in October he was brought back to England and invalided out of the Army. He must have had a tremendous constitution for he continued to live, in somewhat straitened circumstances, until his death on 31 December 1891, from bronchitis. He is buried in Kirkdale Cemetery, Section 17/220.

Postscript

The 1881 Census shows a William Connolly, aged about 60, a widower and Army Pensioner, living as a lodger with the Dove family at 40 Seacombe Street, Everton, Liverpool. Seacombe Street was off Great Homer Street, Liverpool, not very far from Connolly's address at the time of his death. There is a record of the marriage of a William Connolly registered in September 1839 in Liverpool, and this may be our man. Sid Lindsay, presumably by reference to Connolly's death certificate, found that at the time of his death in 1891 William Connolly VC was living at 14 Westminster Road, Liverpool; the 1891 Census, however, locates

William Connolly, a pauper, in the West Derby Union Workhouse at Kirkdale; local historians are of the opinion that this workhouse was situated in Westminster Road and included Number 14. It seems likely, therefore, that John Kirk was another hero who died in obscurity, a pauper in a workhouse.

On 9 February 1886, two Victoria Crosses appeared at auction in London. Lot 218 was that awarded to Gunner William Connolly, Bengal Horse Artillery, for gallantry at Jhelum on 7 July 1857. Spink, the well-known coin and medal dealers, bought it for £10.00! It is now on permanent display in the British India Museum at Colne, Lancashire. However, reports have it that on 16 February 2005 the museum confirmed that the VC in their possession had been tested by Spink 'some years ago' and was declared a fake. The museum does not have any of Connolly's other medals. Over the years, Spink's medal specialists have bought and sold over 300 VCs, many by auction or via fixed price lists, but many more have been by private treaty. Interestingly one of their most recent sales, on 30 April 2004, was the VC awarded to Sergeant N.C.Jackson, RAF for £230,000. Jackson's VC was one of a group of eight of his medals.

$\mathcal{F}$rederick Whirlpool VC

F rederick Whirlpool was born in Liverpool about 1829, the son of Major and Mrs Conker. His father was said to be the Postmaster at Dundalk, Ireland, but a request there for further information received no reply and there are no other details of his earlier life. It appears that he had some sort of disagreement with his father and assumed the surname Whirlpool (possibly because this was a word which his father often used to describe Frederick's somewhat erratic behaviour). We know that he enlisted and was attested in Glasgow on the 23 and 24 October 1854 in the Honourable East India Company's Infantry. He was then described as 'aged 23, 5'7" tall, grey eyes, light brown hair and fresh complexion, a native of Liverpool '. He was sent to the 'John' Company at Warley, Essex, on 28 October 1854 and embarked on the *Salamanca* on 30 November that year, arriving in Bombay on 26 March 1855, where he was posted as Pte 2200 to the 3rd Bombay Fusiliers.

Whirlpool's Regiment is also referred to as the 3rd Bombay European Regiment (109th). It was the third regiment to be numbered 109 and later became the 2nd Battalion, The Prince of Wales Leinster Regiment, which was disbanded after the 1914-18 war. Raised in Poona in 1853 from the 1st Bombay Fusiliers, the 2nd Bombay Light Infantry and recruits from the East India Company's depot at Warley, the regiment joined the Central India Field Force under Sir Hugh Rose in December 1857. It received a baptism of fire at the capture of the fort at Ratgur and took part in action at Barodia, the relief of Sangor and in six other significant battles of the Mutiny.

Jhansi, considered to be the fortress stronghold of the rebels, was also the scene of the most vicious atrocities perpetrated by the rebels against the English. Enormous hatred was displayed during what was seen as wanton barbarity. Thus there was every reason to seek to capture Jhansi and punish the offenders. On 20 March 1858 Sir Hugh Rose sent in his cavalry and artillery to lay siege to the town, followed the next morning by his main force. Rose halted his troops about a mile and a half outside of the town to reconnoitre the area. Between the open ground where he had halted his troops and the town and fortress of Jhansi were the ruined bungalows and houses which, only months before, had been occupied by European families. Together with other service buildings, these were now in varying stages of demolition. The great fort at Jhansi stood on an elevated rock. Built of massive masonry, it had many elaborate outworks of the same solid granite construction and commanded a view across the town and its surrounding area. The town and fortress were garrisoned by 11,000 men, mostly Sipahis (Sepoys), fanatically intent on destroying the Europeans. As the siege was set by Rose's forces, the rebels replied with incessant fire from musket and cannon.

The siege continued, and Rose made plans to storm the fortress walls after setting up a considerable bombardment. Rose's men had to use long ladders to scale the walls and these came under murderous enemy fire as they were put into position. Bitter fighting took place as the walls were scaled and then breached at great cost in terms of casualties. After a siege of 17 days, Jhansi fell. From here, Rose made for Lohari and again after a fierce battle drove out the rebels. It was almost incredible that the British forces were able to fight as well as they did considering the gruelling marches they had made to reach their objectives in a hostile country.

At the battles of Jhansi on 3 April and Lohari on 2 May Frederick Whirlpool showed the kind of commitment that had regularly been shown by Rose's troops. He was awarded his Victoria Cross, announced in the *London Gazette* on 21 October 1859:

> *Frederick Whirlpool, Private, 3rd Bombay European Regiment. Dates of acts of bravery: 3rd April and 2nd May 1858. For gallantly volunteering on the 3rd April, in the attack on Jhansi, to return and carry away several killed and wounded, which he did twice under a very heavy fire from the wall; also for devoted bravery at the assault on Lohari on the 2nd May 1858, in rushing to the rescue of Lieutenant Donne, of the Regiment, who was dangerously wounded. In this service, Private Whirlpool received seventeen desperate wounds, one of which nearly severed his head from his body. The gallant example shown by this man is considered to have greatly contributed to the success of the day.*

An article by Peter Stanley in the *Journal of the Australian War Memorial* in 1984, mentions a somewhat suspect story - that while being carried from the field to the regimental surgeon, Whirlpool said to those carrying him: 'Take care, lads! Don't shake my head or else it will come off!' He spent five months in hospital after which, not surprisingly, he was invalided from the Service on 2 February 1859.

What happened after that is unclear but he did go to Australia and was the first to have his medal presented to him on Australian soil. The occasion selected for the presentation was the annual review of the Volunteers and military forces of the colony of Victoria by the Governor, Sir Henry Barkly, on Thursday 20 June 1861, the date to which the Queen's birthday had been postponed that year following the death of HRH the Duchess of Kent. A public holiday was observed, the weather was exceptionally fine and the review was subsequently described as the most successful ever held in the colony.

On parade for the review were 2,072 troops who, after some parade-ground drill, formed columns, then marched to form three sides of a square. Sir Henry then led Lady Barkly and several other ladies present into the open side. By this time, Whirlpool had enlisted in the Hawthorn and Kew Rifle Volunteers and was present on parade as one of its members. He was then summoned from the ranks and the Deputy Adjutant, Lt Col Carey, read out a General Order from Headquarters, Melbourne, which included Whirlpool's citation. Lady Barkly then stepped forward and fastened the decoration on his breast. The volunteers and spectators cheered and raised their caps on bayonet points. Whirlpool thanked Lady Barkly and returned to his place in the ranks.

As is often the case, Whirlpool's life attracted interest only after his death. It now seems that after his arrival in Australia, he applied for and was awaiting a position with the Victoria Police. Following the receipt of his medal, and possibly with the assistance of the Australian authorities, he again changed his name by deed poll to Frederick Humphrey James and in 1864 left Victoria to live in New South Wales. In 1865 he took charge of a new school, as a teacher for the New South Wales Board of National Education, near Wiseman's Ferry on the Hawkesbury River, north of Sydney. However, allegations of impropriety were made against him by the school secretary with whom he had fallen out. The parents of the pupils supported Whirlpool but the allegations were accepted and in 1867 he was dismissed. This would have left him with only his £10 annual pension as a VC holder and several applications for other teaching posts were rejected. Whirlpool then began to live as a recluse in a slab hut near Windsor, New South Wales, visited only by a Scottish immigrant who had befriended him. It is probable that he died of a heart attack between 23 and 27 June 1899, his body only being found when his weekly groceries were delivered.

He was buried in the Presbyterian cemetery at Windsor, but the location of his grave has since been lost. To quote Peter Stanley: 'The circumstances of his enlistment, the care he took to conceal his fame and the solitude of his later life, hint at a man who may have been ill at ease both with himself and with others. His life - what we know of it - reminds us that in several senses those who receive the Victoria Cross are not like their fellows'.

Postscript

Whirlpool's VC was purchased by Mr Denis Croll. On Croll's death, his widow presented the medal to the Australian War Memorial trustees. The medal is of great significance in Australia as it was the very first to be presented on Australian soil. The Australian War Memorial in Canberra includes a museum and Whirlpool's is one of 59 VCs on display in the Hall of Valour there, the largest publicly held collection of VCs in the world. There is an individual display for each holder, with a photograph, an excerpt from the citation which accompanied the award and usually additional medals awarded to the same individual.

*C*harles Anderson VC

C harles Anderson was a man whose early history is almost unknown. He is believed to have been born in Liverpool in 1826 but his parentage, origins and early life are a mystery. In the notes of Canon Lummis MC (Lummis is acknowledged as an authority on the Victoria Cross) there is mention of a connection with Waterford in Ireland, but enquiries there have so far drawn a blank. His Regimental Museum in Cardiff has no information on him other than his citation.

Anderson enlisted in the 2nd Dragoon Guards (The Queen's Bays) as a private and served in the Indian Mutiny; it was in this campaign that his name was added to those of a very select band of heroes.

In 1858 Sir Colin Campbell, having taken little military action during the very hot weather, determined that during the coming winter the Province of Oudh should be totally subjugated. The River Gogra, running through the province, divided it into two parts, north and south. The southern portion was further divided by the road from Cawnpore to Lucknow and each portion was designated a separate theatre of operations. The southern sections were to be attacked first and simultaneously, and any mutineer fleeing across the Gogra northwards would be attacked in the final phase of the plan.

In October 1858 the operations began, precipitated when the enemy, some 12,000 strong and with artillery support, advanced on the British post at Sundeela, in the eastern portion south of the Gogra. On 6 October the members of the garrison at Sundeela had locked themselves inside the fort and were besieged by the rebels. There was some temporary relief when a small force led by Major Maynard managed to drive the enemy off, but their massive numbers could not be held in check for long. On 8 October a strong brigade from

Lucknow moved up in support. Led by Brigadier Barker, this brigade immediately engaged the enemy and a fierce battle ensued in which no quarter was given by either side. The enemy was completely routed and withdrew.

During this battle, a party of the Queen's Bays was suddenly attacked by 40 rebels, who had been hiding in a dense jungle of sugar cane. The British, under the command of Lt Col Seymour CB, were fired upon at short range before the rebels rushed at them with swords drawn. The Colonel shot the leading rebel with his pistol and discharged the remaining shots into the mutineers but was then himself cut down by two heavy blows from a sword. Seeing their Colonel in this terrible plight, surrounded by the enemy, Pte Charles Anderson and Trumpeter Monaghan at once rushed to his side, with Monaghan shooting one rebel just as he took another swing with his sword. Notwithstanding the tremendous odds against them, the two men held the enemy at bay, enabling Col Seymour to regain his feet. The three then drove the rebels out of the sugar cane. Their gallant and timely rescue of Col Seymour earned both men the Victoria Cross, although they were not gazetted until 11 November 1862, some four years later.

There is a photograph of Charles Anderson, taken by a man named Winter of the city of Waterford, which shows Anderson with his Victoria Cross and another medal, probably the Indian Mutiny medal. It is possible that this photograph was taken when the Regiment was serving in Ireland (it would obviously be after 1862).

Pte Charles Anderson was subsequently promoted to Corporal but no further record of his army service has been found. His Victoria Cross was at some stage purchased and deposited in the United Services Museum in London, with a replica displayed in the Regimental Museum in Cardiff. [A number of websites state that *the* medal is on display in the Queen's Dragoon Guards Regimental Museum, Cardiff, with that of Trumpeter Monaghan and four of the five other VCs earned by the Regiment.]

On 19 April 1899 a report appeared in the *Sunderland Echo* announcing that:

> *This morning the dead body of an old man which has since been identified as that of Charles Anderson, 70 years of age, a miner, was found at the bottom of a large cliff in a garden situated in the lower reaches of Dawdon Dene, belonging to Mr H.B.Wright, solicitor, of*

Seaham Harbour. It is presumed he fell from the cliff. Deceased lodged
with Mr William Stokoe, who lives at Swinebank Cottages.

Anderson's death certificate states that he was 73 years old, a coal miner; the
mines at Seaham were owned by the Marquis of Londonderry and his family,
who also owned the colliers which sailed from Seaham Harbour. Anderson had
died of a fractured skull resulting from an accidental fall over a cliff in Seaham
Dene. He was buried in Princess Road Cemetery, Seaham (Section A, Grave
Number 1271). The service was conducted by the Reverend Copley. There are
no other recorded details of this lonely old man who apparently never married,
nor did he have many friends or relatives.

Postscript

During Sid Lindsey's enquiries into Anderson in 1988, Seaham Council were
alerted to the presence of Charles Anderson's grave in the cemetery. Sid also took
the matter up with the Queen's Dragoons to try to obtain some form of
recognition for this brave but solitary man. The response of the Council was
highly commendable in that they made arrangements to obtain a suitable
headstone. The service of dedication on 14 December 1989 was conducted by
Canon Paul Jobson, Vicar of Seaham, and was attended by the Mayor
(Councillor Ernie Collinson). Captain Richard W.Annan, VC, who earned his
Victoria Cross while serving with the Durham Light Infantry in Belgium in 1940,
represented the Victoria Cross and George Cross Association. Major
K.McMillan, Regimental Secretary of the Queen's Dragoons Old Comrades
Association, placed a wreath on the grave. Sixty people, many of them from the
Regimental Association, turned out on a wet and cold day to pay tribute to this
forgotten hero. L/Cpl Alan Withers, from the small military detachment present,
sounded the *Last Post*.

Sid Lindsay attended the ceremony, but it was typical of his retiring character
that he so played down his part in securing a headstone for Anderson's grave. He
was also instrumental in procuring a headstone in Allerton Cemetery for George
Nurse VC and there are other instances which will be mentioned as we reach
them in this or subsequent books.

George Hinckley VC

Born in Liverpool on 22 June 1819, George Hinckley was the son of a butcher: there are no other details available of his parents or where exactly in Liverpool he was born. It is possible that he joined the Navy in his teens, but the first record of him is as a crewmember of the convict transport ship *Tortoise* at Hobart, Tasmania in February 1842, when he was 22 years of age. It is not known how he came to be in Hobart, although he could have been on a merchant ship and decided this was a quicker way home. He served on other Naval vessels before joining the sloop, HMS *Sphinx*.

The *Sphinx*, a paddle ship of 1,056 tons, built in 1846 at Woolwich, remained in service until 1870 when she was laid up at Plymouth and eventually broken up at Devonport in 1881. She was to serve in the East Indies, was involved in the second Burma War in 1852 and then sailed to the Mediterranean where she took part in the bombardment of Sebastopol on 11 October 1854. In 1859 she returned to the East Indies and the China coast where she stayed until posted to the North America and West Indies station in 1870. It was while on the China Coast that the *Sphinx* was called into the war against the Taiping rebels in 1862. This was one of a number of uprisings which occurred over a period of twenty years, involving opium smugglers, foreign merchants and their respective armed forces and the Chinese ruling powers.

The *Sphinx*, together with HMS *Encounter*, HMS *Flamer* and HMS *Hardy*, landed a force of bluejackets as a naval brigade, to join up with 3,000 men of the Chinese Imperial Army, and 500 men of a French-Chinese naval force. Together, they set off to march the 30 miles from the coast to the fortified town of Fungwha, some 85 miles due south of Shanghai in the Province of Chekiang.

They marched overnight, carrying three days' rations of biscuit and salt pork as well as their ammunition, through the misery of a continuous downpour which had soaked them completely by the time they came within striking distance of the town. It was an appalling journey over rough roads with little sense of direction in the dark, wet night. On arrival at about 4.00am, they camped, had breakfast and were given a tot of rum and by 8.00am were ready to assault the main gates of the fortress. The rebels were well prepared for this attack and subjected the attackers to withering fire from a host of assorted weapons and very soon the area surrounding the town was littered with dead and wounded. The main force withdrew to regroup. In front of the main gate amongst the many casualties were Mr Croker, the Assistant Master of the *Sphinx*, and a Captain Bruman, of the Imperial Chinese Army. Both men were badly wounded and lying out on open ground which was frequently raked by gunfire from the walls of the town. Hinckley asked for permission to rescue at least these two men, ran to Croker, lifted him onto his shoulder and carried him back some 150 yards to shelter. He then ran back a second time, rescuing Captain Bruman similarly, each time running the gauntlet of almost certain death from enemy gunfire. This was the morning of 9 October 1862 and it was to be a further two days before Fungwha was captured.

Able Seaman George Hinckley of HMS *Sphinx* was gazetted on 6 February 1863 to receive the Victoria Cross for his gallant conduct. He received his Cross from the Commander-in-Chief Plymouth, Admiral Houston Stewart, at a ceremony at Mount Wise, Devonport.

Hinckley was a tough naval type, almost fearless, and had suffered the hand of authority for some of his misdemeanours. In 1862, for example, he was rated second-class because of misconduct in January that year, serving 28 days in Hong Kong gaol in May - this was the year he earned his Victoria Cross, more than making amends for his earlier misbehaviour! At the beginning of 1863 he was promoted to Leading Seaman and in July that year he was again promoted to the rank of Quartermaster. He retired from the Navy with that rank in 1867 at the age of 43 years.

In 1865, he had married Jane Oliver, a farmer's daughter, at the parish church of Stoke Damerel in Devon. They had a daughter, Jane Frances, who was born in Garden Street, Moricetown, Devonport, in 1866. By this time Hinckley had changed his name to George Oliver Hinckley, incorporating his wife's maiden name. There is no information as to what occupation he followed after the Navy, but he lived in Devonport for the rest of his life until his death on 31 December 1904 at 44, North Street, Plymouth. Census returns for 1871, 1881, 1891 and 1901 all show Hinckley, described as a 'naval pensioner', living at various addresses in Stoke Damerel. They also show that there were other children in addition to Jane - George R., a son, born 1869 and Rosina, a daughter, born 1868. In the 1901 Census he is shown as having been born in Plymouth, although the rest show his place of birth as Liverpool. His wife, Jane, died on 13 July 1917 aged 88 years, when she was living at 35, Kent Road, in the Ford district of Plymouth. George Hinckley VC is buried in Ford Park Cemetery, Plymouth, and it is interesting to note that his death certificate actually records the fact that he held the Victoria Cross, a mark of respect that was denied most of the others.

Finally, one source states that Hinckley, after receiving his VC in July 1863, lost it at a funeral which he attended in November that year and had to pay 24 shillings for a replacement! On 10 November 1988 at Sotheby's, this official replacement medal was auctioned and sold for £3,300. It, and possibly his original medal, is somewhere in private hands and not on public display.

Paul Aloysius Kenna
VC, DSO

[Note: My intention when undertaking the editing of Sid Lindsey's research notes was to follow them as closely as possible. I have tried my best to do so but in the cases of Paul Aloysius Kenna VC and Gabriel Coury VC, I have had the benefit of reading articles published in the Journal of the Victoria Cross Association and The Stonyhurst Magazine, written by John Mulholland who kindly supplied me with copies of both articles. I have therefore attempted to follow Sid but to amend and supplement his notes by reference to John's articles. W. Sergeant]

Paul Kenna was born at Oakfield House, 22 Richmond Terrace, Everton, Liverpool, on 16 August 1862, the second son of James and Julia Kenna. He was the fourth born of their six children. (*The Register of the Victoria Cross*, 3rd Ed, 1997, gives his date of birth as 2 February 1862.) Both parents came originally from County Meath, Ireland, his father from Ballinakill House in that county. James Kenna had settled in Liverpool to work as a broker and cattle dealer. Also living at the family home were James's elder brother, Patrick, described as a landowner, and his unmarried sister, Teresa, and the family enjoyed the luxury of two resident servants. James was 13 years older than his wife and died unexpectedly on a visit to France on 6 December 1873, aged 51 years. Prior to his death, the family lived quietly and comfortably in Liverpool, and John Mulholland points out that on his death James left £44,000 in his will, a substantial amount even today. The newly widowed Julia Kenna moved her family to Ramsgate.

They were devout Roman Catholics, and at the age of seven Paul was sent to

St Francis Xavier School, Shaw Street, Liverpool, moving to St Augustine's Abbey School in Ramsgate in September 1874. Although not a particularly gifted boy academically, Kenna worked hard and is said to have been fiercely competitive, especially on the sports field. He was also noted as a very devout boy and it was no surprise when in 1879 he moved on to Stonyhurst College, the Jesuit public school in Lancashire. He was well liked by his contemporaries and was an energetic and enthusiastic sportsman and at the end of his schooling decided on an Army career. Again, John Mulholland describes how while at Stonyhurst, to the amusement of his fellows, Kenna grew a military-style moustache. He left the school in 1881 and went to live with his uncle in County Durham, being commissioned as a Lieutenant in a Militia Battalion of the Durham Light Infantry. He resigned his commission and qualified for entry to the Royal Military College, Sandhurst in 1885.

In 1886, Kenna was granted a commission as a 2nd Lt in the 2nd Battalion of the West India Regiment, subsequently serving in the West Indies and in West Africa. In 1889, he transferred to the 21st Hussars, later to be known as the 21st (Empress of India's) Lancers. From 1890 until 1895, the 21st Lancers were stationed in India, where Kenna established himself as an expert horseman, especially off-duty when he took part in chasing, hunting and polo. It is likely that this was encouraged by the Army authorities as the Regiment was not stationed near any trouble spots and such activities fostered a spirit of competitiveness and teamwork. In 1893 and 1894, Kenna was the leading gentleman-rider in India and his modest and sociable nature made him welcome wherever he went.

In the early summer of 1895 Kenna spent some leave with relatives in Ireland and on 8 June rescued a man who had jumped into the River Liffey in Dublin and for this he was awarded the Royal Humane Society's 'Vellum Testimonial'. (Mulholland recounts how in later years Kenna bemoaned the fact that while effecting the rescue, his purse and watch were stolen from his jacket.) On 12 June 1895 he was promoted to the rank of Captain and was clearly rising in society, for in July that year he married Lady Cecilia Josephine Bertie, daughter of the 7th Earl of Abingdon. Tragically, however, Cecilia died of typhoid fever within months.

In 1896, the 21st Lancers went to Egypt to relieve the 2nd Dragoon Guards and during this tour of duty Kenna earned his Victoria Cross. This campaign stemmed from the slaughter in 1885 of the British Governor of the Sudan,

General Charles Gordon, killed at Khartoum by the fanatical followers of Mohammed Ahmed (the Mahdi), who claimed descent from Mohammed. The death of Gordon caused a tremendous public outcry in Britain and the Prime Minister, William Gladstone, withdrew the British forces from the Sudan, leaving the country and its inhabitants to the cruel regime of the Mahdi and his successor, the Khalifa. The Sudan had been a part of Egyptian sovereign territory with a great number of British officers and other officials being employed in its administration. Such was the terror and oppression over the next ten years under the fanatics that the population diminished from eight million to two million.

In March 1896, an Anglo-Egyptian Expeditionary Force was planned, with Major General Sir Herbert Kitchener in command, with the intention of marching on Khartoum and deposing the Khalifa and his followers. This was an enormous project involving the movement of some 26,000 men with their equipment, horses, camels and artillery, together with the necessary supplies to service them. It took almost two years to get this army within striking distance of Khartoum, which is over 1000 miles from Cairo. In September 1898, the force made camp about four miles from Omdurman, a town just north of the capital, Khartoum. Not far away, the Khalifa sent out his fanatical warriors to attack Kitchener's force. Although the attackers numbered 4000, their first attack was repulsed and Kitchener prepared to advance on Omdurman to deny the enemy a base. The terrain was an almost barren expanse crossed by ridges; these gave cause for great concern, as it was impossible to determine the strength or disposition of the enemy.

Early on the morning of 2 September, the 21st Lancers, under the command of Col R. H. Martin, were ordered to advance over rising ground between a prominent hill and the River Nile. Kitchener's orders were that they should advance and harass the enemy's flank and attempt to head them off from Omdurman. Col Martin sent out two patrols to scout ahead, but was informed that there was a group of a few hundred Dervishes intent on blocking their advance. He did not see this as much of an obstacle to his 400 Lancers and unwisely took up the challenge, not realising that this was an old Arab ploy. His men advanced at a gallop, rapidly gathering pace and the distance shortened as the order was given to 'Charge!'. As the Lancers braced themselves, there arose from the ridges on their flank some 3000 white-robed Dervishes. The trap had been sprung; the Lancers could not turn back and were now suffering from enemy gunfire. There was only one course open to them - to wheel the galloping Lancers into line and allow the impetus of the charge to carry them back through the enemy on their flank. That they managed this at all was due to magnificent horsemanship and the enemy was quickly in disarray as the Lancers literally cut their way through the screaming fanatics despite their own heavy losses. The tribesmen made the Lancers' horses their first target and many were killed, leaving their riders to fight for their lives, desperately trying to hack their way through the massed ranks of the enemy. Meanwhile, those still mounted had safely made their way back to the ridge, eager and ready to charge through the Dervishes again. The Colonel would not allow a second charge in view of the serious losses sustained in the first. Dismounting, the Lancers subjected the tribesmen to a withering carbine enfilade and as this took effect, the Dervishes drew back and retreated - more than 2000 were repelled by 300 Lancers. The Lancers had been divided into four Squadrons, A, B, C and D, with Kenna as second in command to Major Fowle in A Squadron. One of his four troop leaders was Lt de Montmorency, and Winston Churchill was a lieutenant in the 4th Hussars, attached to A Squadron.

It is generally agreed that Kenna and B Squadron went in where the enemy was most densely packed and this is borne out by the fact that his squadron won all of the three VCs awarded that day and was the only one to have an officer killed.

Major W.G.Crole-Wyndham, second-in-command of the 21st Lancers to Col Martin, was at the head of the initial charge, when his horse was killed beneath him, pitching forward and dislodging him amongst the Dervishes but somehow he rolled clear. Kenna, following behind him, stopped his horse allowing Crole-Wyndham to mount behind him while he used a revolver to hold off the Dervishes. Unfortunately, Kenna's horse took exception to this additional weight and threw them after only 50 yards. Both men landed on their feet and while Kenna retrieved his horse, Cole-Wyndham was able to escape on foot. Both rejoined the line. As John Mulholland recounts, subsequent commentators tended to minimise Kenna's part in this rescue, Churchill for instance not even mentioning Kenna in his account.

Meanwhile, the action was still in progress. Lt Grenfell, another of the troop leaders, was unseated when his horse was wounded and then he himself was hacked to death by Dervish swords. Lt de Montmorency, one of Kenna's best friends, unaware that Grenfell was dead, went to his aid. He shot dead a Dervish horseman who was chasing Crole-Wyndham as he made his escape and then, inflamed by the carnage about him and especially seeing the mutilated bodies of British Lancers, de Montmorency charged at any Dervish in sight. Accompanied by Kenna and Corporal Swarbrick, he tried to recover the corpse of Lt Grenfell, but his horse bolted, leaving him to the mercy of the enemy. Kenna and Swarbrick chased after the horse while he stood guard over Grenfell's body. Returning with the horse, Kenna and Swarbrick again attempted to lift Grenfell but were unable to do so and rode back to the Regiment.

The merits and otherwise of the decision to attack taken by Colonel Martin have been debated since. Five officers and 65 men of the Lancers were killed and wounded, compared with no more than 60 or 70 Dervish casualties. However, it should be remembered that many thousands of fanatics were killed during the initial battle preceding the charge - somewhat to the embarrassment if not shame of commentators because of the ease of such slaughter.

One aspect which is not in dispute, however, is the bravery of many officers and men. Three Victoria Crosses were awarded : to Captain Kenna, to Lt de Montmorency and to Pte Byrne, his servant. Many other awards were made to Lancers, including the Distinguished Conduct Medal to Cpl Swarbrick.

Kenna's VC was gazetted in 1898 and on 6 January 1899 at Osborne House, he received his Cross from Queen Victoria. Invested at the same ceremony were de Montmorency, Byrne and Lt N.M.Smyth of the 2nd Dragoon Guards, who also won his award at Omdurman.

While Kenna was being feted at Stonyhurst and elsewhere, the storm-clouds were gathering in South Africa. Kenna was appointed Assistant Provost Marshal to the Cavalry Division under Sir John French and on 22 October 1899 sailed for South Africa. He was quickly involved in action near Colesburg, for which he was mentioned in despatches by French. In 1900 he was promoted to Major, fighting at the relief of Kimberley and elsewhere, including the Zululand frontier in Natal and Somaliland in the campaign to oust the 'Mad Mullah'.

John Mulholland gives this account of an episode in the Somaliland campaign: on 19 December 1903, withdrawing from a position, troops under Kenna's command were followed by enemy horsemen. During the retirement, Pte Jai Singh of the Poona Mounted Infantry lost his horse and was closely pursued by a large number of the enemy. Lt H.A.Carter, attached to the 6th Poona Mounted Infantry, rode back alone for 400 yards, took Singh on his horse and carried him to safety. Kenna, in his report, described this as 'the finest and most brilliant act of valour performed in the Somali Campaign', and recommended Carter for the Victoria Cross. This was downgraded to a DSO, announced in the *London Gazette* of 7 June 1904. When Kenna returned to England, he took up the case with the authorities and the decision was reversed. Carter's VC was announced on 9 December 1904. Clearly, Kenna was determined that Carter should get the award he deserved.

De Montmorency and Byrne had by now joined Kenna in South Africa but in February 1900, de Montmorency was killed by a Boer sniper – this was witnessed by Byrne who had to be physically restrained from attempting to recover the body. During the Boer War, Kenna earned promotion to Brevet Major and was awarded a Distinguished Service Order (making him only the second Army officer to hold both the VC and DSO, the first being Captain F.A.Maxwell), the Queen's Medal with six clasps and the King's Medal with two clasps.

Kenna returned to England and on 2 March 1905 remarried, his new wife being Angela Mary, daughter of the late Hubert Titchbourne Hibbert, of Beaufort Gardens, London. The wedding took place at the Brompton Oratory, Kensington with a Guard of Honour provided by a body of troopers from the 21st Lancers. They had two daughters - Kathleen born in 1906 and Cecilia born in 1909. At the time of writing, Cecilia is still alive and attended the unveiling of the Victoria Cross and George Cross Memorial at Westminster Abbey in May 2003. Kathleen died childless in 1998.

On 1 December 1906 Kenna was appointed aide de camp to King Edward VII. He retired from his command and from the Army on 7 September 1910, after 24 years of active and loyal service. In April 1912, however, as the situation in Europe began to deteriorate, he was appointed to command the Notts and Derby (Yeomanry) Mounted Brigade. At this time he was living at North Kilworth Hall, near Rugby, regularly attended Church and was the patron of the local Boy Scouts Troop. When war broke out in August 1914, Kenna was in Europe, taking part in an exhibition of horsemanship. He met the British Expeditionary Force, returning to this country to join up with his Brigade as Brigadier-General, forming part of the Midlands Mounted Division under Major General Peyton.

In April 1915, the Division landed in Egypt, just six days before the landings at Gallipoli, widely considered to have been one of the most tragic mistakes of the War. The defence of this peninsula by the Turks was fierce and unremitting, causing hundreds of Allied casualties. In August 1915 further landings were planned and on 18 August the Midlands Mounted Division arrived at Suvla Bay. Major General Peyton left to command the 9th Corps and Brigadier Kenna assumed his command. After 60 hours of fighting as infantrymen, no doubt much to Kenna's chagrin, his men were forced back to the slopes of Chocolate Hill. Here, on 29 August, as he carried out a forward inspection of his lines, Kenna was shot by a Turkish sniper, the bullet passing through his arm and into his chest. In great pain, he knew he was dying and called for a priest. He passed away in the early hours of 30 August 1915 and is buried at Lala Baba Cemetery, south of Suvla Bay.

A great soldier and a devout Christian, Paul Aloysius Kenna loved his country, the Army, his family and his horses. To the medals listed earlier were added the 1914-15 Star, British War Medal, Victory Medal with oak-leaf for Mention in Despatches, the 1902 and 1911 Coronation Medals and the Khedive's Sudan Medal. In the 1980s, Kenna's decorations and medals were donated by his daughters to the Queen's Royal Lancers Regimental Museum in Belvoir Castle where they are on display today.

Ernest Wright Alexander
VC, CB, CMG

Ernest Wright Alexander was born on 20 October 1870, the son of Robert and Annie Alexander, at 'Devonshire', Princes Park, Liverpool. (Some records show him as born on 2 October.) *Gore's Directory* for 1870 shows Robert Alexander, a ship owner, living at 38 Devonshire Road, Princes Park, Liverpool. Robert was a prominent ship owner and merchant who had settled in Liverpool from Belfast. His mother was the daughter of James Cramton Gregg, also of Belfast. The firm of Robert Alexander & Co had established the Sun

Shipping Company, with offices at 17 Water Street, Liverpool, in 1868. This later became the very successful Hall Line of steamers. In 1901, because of Robert's ill health and the fact that his other sons, Arthur and Frederick, although members of the family business, were too inexperienced to ensure its continuing success, Robert sold the business to J.R.Ellerman for the sum of £434,000. The Hall Line name was retained until the 1960s and was a significant contributor to the success of the Ellerman shipping company.

Ernest, who was educated at Cherbourg House, Malvern, and later at Harrow, chose to go direct from school to the Royal Military Academy, where he embarked on an impressive military career. He was appointed 2nd Lt in the Royal Artillery on 27 June 1889; promoted to Captain in the Royal Field Artillery on 26 December 1899, serving in India from September 1892 until November 1900 and again between October 1903 and June 1906; and just before he left India in 1906 was promoted within the Royal Artillery to the rank of Major. On 1 September 1903 he married Rose, the daughter of the late Major H.G.Newcombe, Royal Artillery, who was formerly in the Royal Bodyguard. Twins were born in 1905 and were named after their paternal grandparents, Robert and Annie. A son, George William, was born in 1911 and later a daughter, Mary.

War against Germany was declared at midnight on 4 August 1914 and the first detachment of the British Expeditionary Force (BEF) landed in France on 12 August. By 18 August practically the whole of the BEF had been landed and concentrated in the area of Valenciennes and the town of Maubeuge. From there, they began to move into position, never suspecting the bloody onslaught which was to follow. The 2nd Army Corps under Lt Gen Sir Horace Smith-Dorrien occupied a line along the canal from Condé through to Mons and then out to Oberg, a distance of 23 miles, covered by the 3rd and 5th Divisions. Ten battalions took up a forward position in an attempt to stem the steamroller-like advance of six German Divisions. So commenced the Battle of Mons on 23 August.

In the vicinity of Elouges, a little to the south-west of Mons, the British flank guard was positioned. Here, the 1st Bn the Cheshire Regiment, with the 1st Bn the Norfolk Regiment, supported by artillery and a party of cavalry, faced the entire German IV Army Corps. As a result of the impetus and the numerical superiority of the enemy against such a thin line of resistance on the main front, a controlled withdrawal was ordered. The success of this manoeuvre was contingent upon the ability of the flank guard to hold position. The determination of those involved was never in doubt, for the one factor which had confounded the Germans during their advance was the sheer professionalism of the BEF. One of the artillery units supporting the flank guard was 119 Battery, Royal Field Artillery, commanded by Major Ernest Wright Alexander.

The Battle of Elouges began around noon on 24 August 1914. The enemy had not reckoned with the tenacious resistance offered by the flank guard, and although they outnumbered the defenders by six to one and their artillery was firing at a rate 20 times faster than the British guns, their advance was drastically slowed and they sustained terrible losses. As large numbers of German infantry were mowed down, however, ever more came on, and the British position weakened as casualties mounted. With dead and wounded men and horses everywhere, it was only the desperate fight for survival that sustained the morale of the remaining troops. Major Alexander, already acknowledged to be a dedicated gunnery officer, was determined to keep his guns in action as long as there were men to fire them, but as the Germans advanced he realised that he must take steps to ensure that his guns did not fall into enemy hands.

To Alexander's left were some Lancers, survivors of a charge which had attempted to draw the attack away from the infantry. Although they too had suffered heavy losses as they made their way across open terrain, they were now reforming in order to avoid being trapped. They were under the command of Captain Francis Grenfell of the 9th Lancers, who, on seeing Alexander's plight, with all his horses killed and most of his men dead or wounded, came to his assistance to help clear the guns. The ground was soft and not easy to traverse; shells and bullets were flying about in all directions, but the officers and men took on the task of manhandling the guns by means of drag ropes. This would have been no mean feat in ideal conditions and was all but impossible in their current circumstances. Grenfell, although badly wounded in the earlier charge, wasted no time in getting to work on the ropes alongside his men. He and Alexander toiled with and gave encouragement to their men, setting an example in the best tradition of the armed services. The six guns were saved and moved to new positions but the cost of the Battle of Elouges to both sides was horrific. The 1st Bn of the Cheshire Regiment alone suffered as many as 800 casualties of its strength of about 1000. Both Major Ernest Wright Alexander and Captain Francis Grenfell earned their Victoria Crosses at Elouges.

Alexander's citation in the *London Gazette* states:

> *For conspicuous bravery and great ability at Elouges, on 24 August 1914, when the flank guard was attacked by a German Corps, in handling his battery against overwhelming odds with such conspicuous success that all his guns were saved, notwithstanding that they had to be withdrawn by hand by himself and others. This enabled the retirement of the 5th Division to be carried out without very serious loss. Subsequently, Major Alexander rescued a badly wounded man under heavy fire with the greatest gallantry and devotion to duty.*

The Battle of Mons lasted two days and it has been said, which is little consolation, that the total casualties were less than those 100 years earlier at nearby Waterloo. The most significant aspect of Mons was the behaviour and discipline manifested by the British soldiers. Despite being thrown into the heat of battle little more than a week after their arrival in France, they showed immense skill and application in the face of greatly superior numbers. The account they gave of themselves, it has been said, caused General von Kluck and his IV Corps to lose the initiative.

On 30 October 1914, Ernest Alexander was promoted to Lieutenant Colonel, commanding the 22nd Brigade, Royal Field Artillery and later the 27th Brigade. In August 1915 he became Temporary Brigadier General in command of the 15th Divisional Royal Artillery, and early the following year became GOC (Royal Artillery) with the 15th Army Corps, a position which he was to occupy until March 1917, when he was given command of the Royal Artillery 11th Corps. In April 1918, he was appointed Major General (Temporary) at Royal Artillery Headquarters of the First Army. Between 1914 and August 1919, he was Mentioned in Despatches on nine occasions.

He was created a Companion of the Order of St Michael & St George (CMG) in 1915, received the Military Order of Savoy (Cavalier) in 1918; was created a Companion of the Bath (CB) in 1919 and received the Croix de Guerre in the same year. He was also created Grand Officer, Military Order of Avis.

In the *Army List* of 5 June 1919, Alexander is shown as Brigadier General (Temporary), Commander Royal Artillery, Southern Area, Aldershot Command. He retired in 1920 and lived at Horswell House, Kingsbridge, South Devon. He died at his home on 25 August 1934, just 20 years after his act of heroism, at the relatively early age of 64 years, and was buried in Putney Vale Cemetery, London. His wife Rose died just one month later. There is a memorial to both of them in the cemetery, and a road running along the southern boundary of the cemetery is called Alexander Way.

Postscript

The first Victoria Cross of the 1914-18 War was awarded posthumously on 23 August 1914 to Lt Maurice Dease, Royal Fusiliers, at Nimy, north of Mons. This was just 24 hours before the actions in which Alexander and Grenfell won their Crosses. On 25 February 1999, Alexander's VC was sold for around £85,000 and is thought to have been acquired by Lord Ashcroft for his medal collection.

Gabriel George Coury VC

Born on 13 June 1896 at 16 Croxteth Grove, Sefton Park, Liverpool 8, Gabriel was the second son of Raphael and Marie Coury. His father was of Armenian descent, whilst his mother was French. 16 Croxteth Grove would seem to have been the family home, as his grandfather, Basil, also lived there. Basil and Raphael were also listed as cotton merchants in the firm of Coury & Company at 66 The Albany, Old Hall Street, Liverpool. There is no record of this Company being in business, at least under that name, after 1912; the cotton trade was in decline by then.

Gabriel had an older brother, Charles, who was for many years a 'Ring Trader' with the firm of H.W.Hooper and operated directly on the floor of the Cotton Exchange. He also had two younger brothers and two sisters. One brother, Maurice, had been employed in the firm of Reiss Brothers and for a short time held a commission in the Lancashire Fusiliers, but was forced to retire from the Army through ill health. Maurice died, aged 26 years, on 17 April 1926. His other brother, Ernest, was also employed in the cotton trade but died when only 38 years of age on 3 August 1939. Charles died in 1961.

In an article published in the *Stonyhurst Magazine* in 2004, John Mulholland noted that Raphael Coury was a Turkish subject, born in Alexandria, Egypt, while his wife Marie was born in Beirut. Charles and one of Gabriel's elder sisters, Aimée, were born in Alexandria, while the remaining children were born in Liverpool between 1894 and 1900. Raphael and Marie apparently started their married life in Egypt, moving to Liverpool between the birth of Aimée (1892) and Louise Andrée (1894). The 1901 Census shows the family living at 'The Mount', Waterloo Park, Waterloo, employing five female staff – one born in Belgium, one in Georgia, USA and a third in Sidon, Syria – the other two were locals.

Raphael Coury died in 1903 aged only 43 years, leaving his widow to care for six young children. Some time later, Marie, with her two daughters, moved to London, where Louise was to become a journalist on one of the high class glossy magazines, while Aimée, with some help from Charles, accepted responsibility for looking after her mother. Aimée died in March 1950, but her mother survived until November 1957. Marie, Raphael, Aimée, Maurice, Ernest and Gabriel are all buried in the family grave in the churchyard of St Peter and St Paul's, Liverpool Road North, Crosby.

Between 1901 and May 1907, Gabriel Coury was educated at St Francis Xavier (SFX) School, Salisbury Street, Liverpool. SFX School was attached to the Jesuit Church of the same name. In May 1907, with his younger brother Maurice, he started at Stonyhurst College, a leading Roman Catholic independent school run by Jesuits in the Ribble Valley near Blackburn, Lancashire. Celebrated former pupils include Sir Arthur Conan Doyle, Charles Laughton, Lord Devlin and Monsignor Bruce Kent, and the famous Jesuit poet, Gerard Manley Hopkins, taught there. In addition, the College can boast no less than seven former pupils who have earned the Victoria Cross. [Further information may be found in *Seven VCs of Stonyhurst College* by H.L.Kirby and R.R.Walsh.] Although not an outstanding scholar, Gabriel was certainly popular with his peers and enjoyed most sports including football and cricket. If he stood out at all it was because, no doubt due to his mother's influence, he could speak fluent French.

In April 1913, Gabriel left Stonyhurst and took up an apprenticeship with Messrs Reynolds and Gibson, Cotton Merchants and Brokers, in Liverpool. He was doing well, but on 4 August 1914 war was declared and, like many of his contemporaries, he decided to answer the call of duty. He enlisted as a Rifleman in the 2/6th Bn the King's (Liverpool) Regiment. Interestingly, as Kirby and Walsh point out, Coury was the only one of the seven Stonyhurst VCs to actually join the Army in time of war and was the only one to enlist as a private. After his initial training, he applied for and was granted a commission, becoming a 2nd Lt in the 3rd Bn, the South Lancashire Regiment (The Prince of Wales's Volunteers) in April 1915. He arrived in France in August 1915, now attached to the 1/4th Bn of the same regiment, which by this time had been designated a Pioneer battalion. By coincidence, when he found his way to the trenches for the first time, the unit holding the line on his battalion's right was the 2/6th King's, his original unit.

The latter part of 1915 saw minimal action on both sides, mainly because of the adverse weather conditions. As these improved in spring 1916, preparations were put in hand for the offensive which was to become etched into the national memory as the 'Battle of the Somme'. It opened on 1 July 1916, with disastrous loss of life along a 15-mile front involving fifteen British Divisions. It will forever be remembered as the most disastrous start to a planned military campaign, with the young men of Britain being wiped out in their thousands. Towards the end of July, the 55th (West Lancashire) Division TA moved into the line to replace the battle-weary troops in the sector facing the 'dreadful' village of Guillemont – dreadful because of the number of failed attempts to capture it. 2nd Lt Coury was now involved in the onerous duties of pioneering.

The role of the Pioneer is anything but glamorous and the conditions imposed by the war of attrition in the trenches made the job one of the most hazardous in the whole of the front line. The Pioneer undertook a multitude of tasks, usually at night, involving heavy manual labour in wet and muddy trenches, more often than not under fire. At other times, he would be stumbling forward over the shell-pocked quagmire of ground, setting the heavy tripod supports and spreading barbed wire across no man's land, crouching low as enemy flares lit up the sky.

By 28 July, with the initial phases of the Somme operation still in progress, Coury and his men found themselves at Fricourt with companies of his unit working each night in the forward areas around the Briqueterie and Trones Wood. Between 23 July and 3 September 1916 the battle for Guillemont raged. During the first week of August, preparatory to yet another attack, the Pioneers were engaged in digging trenches from Trones Wood towards the village. Coury's unit's casualties increased significantly.

On 5 August, according to the account compiled by Coury's captain, Coury was in a trench during a particularly heavy bombardment, when several shells landed near the trench and ignited a ton of Very Lights. These exploded, causing considerable panic, with some troops attempting to leave the trench, believing the Germans were making a bomb attack. Coury took charge of the situation, picking up a rifle and bayonet, and got the men back into their places. During the bombardment which followed, he patrolled the trench at great risk to himself, restoring confidence and maintaining order.

On 8 August 1916 a further attack on Guillemont was launched. As the first wave of infantrymen went in, they were closely followed by the Pioneers, whose task was to dig communication trenches from newly-won positions back to the original front line. 'D' Company of the 4th Bn South Lancashire Regiment, now attached to 164 Infantry Brigade for this operation, had been divided into two sections, the right half commanded by Captain G.Collingwood and the left under 2nd Lt Gabriel Coury, working respectively with the 1st/8th King's Liverpool Regiment and the 1st/4th King's Own. As they moved forward, the ground was frequently raked by machine gun and artillery fire. To describe the fighting as 'confused' is an understatement but suffice it to say that the attack broke down. In between times, Collingwood's section had dug out 60 yards of trench, whilst Coury's had, in one hour, completed 100 yards of trench, five feet deep, and all in the midst of a raging battle. It was a truly magnificent effort by both sections but only at a great cost – two officers, including Collingwood, were killed, one officer and 47 other ranks wounded and five other ranks reported missing. Despite this, Coury rallied his men and completed the trench. The main attack had failed and the troops were ordered to withdraw, leaving many of their wounded in no man's land. Coury, however, went out to rescue his wounded Commanding Officer, Lt Col J.L.Swainson, returning to organise his shaken troops to fend off an attempted German counterattack. Coury brought Swainson back to safety but Swainson died within two hours of the rescue.

For his deeds, Coury was awarded the Victoria Cross. The *London Gazette* citation reads as follows:

> *During an advance he was in command of two platoons ordered to dig a communication trench from the old firing line to the positions won. By his fine example and utter contempt for danger he kept up the spirits of his men and completed his task under heavy fire. Later, after the Battalion with whom he was working had suffered severe casualties and the Commanding Officer had been wounded, he went out in front of the advanced position, and in full daylight, in full view of the enemy, he found the Commanding Officer and brought him back to safety over ground swept with machine gun fire. He not only completed his original task and then saved the Commanding Officer, but he also succeeded in rallying the attacking troops when they were shaken, and leading them forward.*

Coury was only 20 years of age and was the youngest of the Stonyhurst VCs to receive the award. In late August 1916, Gabriel Coury was promoted to the rank of lieutenant and transferred to the Royal Flying Corps as an observer.

On 18 November, 1916, he received his Victoria Cross from King George V at Buckingham Palace, then left for Liverpool where he was afforded full civic honours. Escorted by Col Sir James Reynolds, Senior Partner in Reynolds and Gibson (Coury's employers before his enlistment), he was led through massed throngs to the Cotton Exchange in Old Hall Street, where he was granted the freedom of the Liverpool Cotton Exchange for life. He was then invited by the Lord Mayor, Councillor Max Muspratt, to a civic reception in the Town Hall, travelling there in the Mayoral coach. After luncheon, the Lord Mayor spoke of the honour that Gabriel Coury had brought to the City, saying: 'When you return to civil life, your influence will be considerably enhanced by the deed you have done, and your example will stand out and make the young men of this city worthier of the great place to which they belong'. An eye-witness account of Coury's exploits featured in the *Liverpool Daily Post* of 30 October 1916:

> *He was the bravest officer I ever served under. He showed absolute contempt for death and made us all feel that a dozen deaths were as nothing compared with the necessity of completing the task given to us. It was when we got into the captured position that Lt.Coury showed what he was capable of. We had gone though a hellish ordeal...a lot of our officers and men lay out there in the open, wounded.... It blew hurricanes of fire across the open and it seemed to invite certain death to go out there. Lt Coury started out under fiendish fire. The enemy's snipers were after him from the first but he ran right on regardless of the hail of bullets flying around him. He started back again, carrying our commander...The journey back was one of the most thrilling sights I have ever seen. The enemy redoubled their efforts to pick off the brave officer as he toiled painfully towards our trench... the enemy's machine guns were turned on full blast and it was nothing short of a miracle that the Lieutenant was able to make his way through it at all.... All were loud in their praise of our Lieutenant. Undoubtedly, he saved the day at its most critical stage.*

Twelve months later, Coury almost lost his life. In atrocious weather, he volunteered to ferry much-needed aeroplanes from the United Kingdom to the front line in France. Heading at low level towards the Channel, his wing struck a flagpole and his plane crashed. The fuel supply ignited and as he lay unconscious he sustained severe burns to his arms, legs and face. An American officer who witnessed the crash was astounded that he had survived. He recovered from his injuries in the Royal Herbert Hospital, Woolwich.

By 7 January 1918, he had recovered sufficiently to marry Katherine Mary Lovell, the only daughter of Stuart and Mary Lovell, manufacturers of sweets and confectionery, of Clapham Common, London. In April Coury returned to flying but in June that year he crashed again. This time, on his discharge from hospital, he was given a desk job with the RAF. He and Katherine had three daughters, all of whom were educated at the Ursuline Convent in Blundellsands.

After the war, Gabriel returned to work for Messrs Reynolds and Gibson, living first at 2, Merton Grove, Bootle, moving in 1926 to 38 Brooke Road, Waterloo. Following in the footsteps of his father, Gabriel went to work on behalf of the company in Alexandria, Egypt. While he and his wife were in Egypt, his three daughters were boarded at school on the Isle of Wight and later at the Ursuline Convent. By 1932, Coury and his wife had returned to England and in 1939, at the outbreak of the Second World War, Gabriel was still on the Army Officers' Reserve List. In January 1940 he enlisted in the Royal Army Service Corps, serving in England until 1944 when he took part in the Normandy landings. He then saw action throughout France, Belgium, Holland and Germany before demobilisation in August 1945.

Stressful as his return to the war-zone in France must have been, his return to 'Civvy Street' was even more traumatic. The new Labour Government decided to retain control of the raw cotton market, causing many smaller companies to close and drastically reducing the number of jobs available within the trade. Coury, as a returning soldier, was entitled to return to his old job but only if it still existed. There *was* no job for him, or for many of his returning comrades.

His next move almost certainly surprised and amazed his friends, if not his family. He decided to open a fish and chip shop at 103, Brunswick Road, Liverpool. Surprising it may have been, but Gabriel applied himself to this new career with the dedication and zeal he had displayed throughout his life. He was a very successful shopkeeper and quickly extended his interests to catering in many of the main public parks in Liverpool, including Reynolds Park, Woolton - formerly the home of his earlier boss, Sir James Reynolds. Although the Cotton Exchange did not reopen as a free market until 1954, Coury had already returned to the trade in 1952, as manager and senior salesman with George Way and Company. His wife looked after the chip shop and catering concessions.

In 1955, his health, which had not been good since 1918, broke down and he spent time in Walton Hospital, Liverpool. At one stage, his condition was so poor that the Last Rites were administered. He improved, however, and returned home, but died on 23 February 1956, aged 59 years. His funeral, two days later, at the Church of St Peter and St Paul, Liverpool Road, Crosby, was attended by over 300 people, including Lt.Col Donald Farmer VC, who earned his medal in the South African War in 1900. Senior representatives from the Army and RAF were there, together with many of his colleagues from the cotton trade. Six National Servicemen from the South Lancashire Regiment carried his coffin, and the service was conducted by staff and pupils from Stonyhurst College.

At a Remembrance Day Service in London on 12 November 1961, his widow, Katherine, presented her husband's Victoria Cross to the Regimental Association of the South Lancashire Regiment for safekeeping. It was held by the Regimental Museum in Warrington. The ceremony took place privately at the Grosvenor Hotel in Victoria, after the members of the Association and their families had planted crosses in the Field of Remembrance in the churchyard of St Margaret's, Westminster, earlier that afternoon. Brigadier H.H.Whalley-Kelly accepted the Cross on behalf of the Regimental Association, and Gabriel Coury's three daughters were in attendance. A portrait of Coury hangs in Stonyhurst College.

Postscript

Coury's medal entitlement was VC, 1914-15 Star, British War Medal, Victory Medal, 1939-45 Star, France and Germany Star, Defence Medal, War Medal, and the 1937 and 1953 Coronation Medals. His 1914-15 Star was exhibited by a private exhibitor at the Annual Convention of the Order and Medals Research Society in London in 1999 but the whereabouts of his other eight medals, apart from his VC, are unknown. John Mulholland, in the *Stonyhurst Magazine*, relates how, on the 26th anniversary of Coury's death on 23 February 1982, the Regimental Museum at Warrington was broken into and two VC displays were stolen. These related to Coury and Colour Sergeant J.Lucas. Fortunately both VCs were copies for display purposes but in the case of Lucas, his New Zealand Campaign and Long Service and Good Conduct Medals were originals. The original of Coury's VC is now held by the Queen's Lancashire Regiment at their museum in Preston.

David Jones VC

David Jones was born on 10 January 1892 at 3, Hutchinson Street, Liverpool 6, at that time in the West Derby district. He was the son of David Jones and his wife, Jessie, née Ginochio. Jessie was the daughter of an Italian, Peter Ginochio, who had arrived in England from Genoa, and Sarah, who was born in Manchester but lived in the famous Italian area of Liverpool off Scotland Road. David Jones (Senior) was at that time employed as a cotton porter and they married in Liverpool in 1885, setting up home in Hutchinson Street with Jessie's mother Sarah. In 1901 they were living at 25, Elmore Street, Everton, Liverpool, and there are now 5 children – Joseph, David (b.1892), William, John A. and Samuel. Another daughter, Marguerette, no longer lived with the family.

Jones was educated at Heyworth Street School, Everton and on leaving took up employment with Blakes' Motor Company, Lord Street, Liverpool, where he trained as a motor mechanic. In those days, of course, he would have been dealing with very new technology. He was a very popular employee and when war broke out in August 1914, he told his employers that he intended to volunteer. With their blessing and before the end of August, he enlisted as a private in the King's Liverpool Regiment.

On 27 May 1915 Jones married Elizabeth Dorothea Doyle, and they made their home at 87 Heyworth Street, Liverpool 5. On his marriage certificate David is described as a coach builder of 27 Aigburth Street, and his father as a carter. They had no family. He displayed the same enthusiasm and commitment to being a soldier as he had shown during his training with Blakes and it was no surprise that he quickly earned promotion. As a sergeant in the 12th Bn of the King's he earned his Victoria Cross during the difficult and costly Battle of the Somme in 1916.

From late July that year, there were a number of attempts to break the enemy's hold on the village of Guillemont. All were repulsed at horrendous cost in terms of lives lost. In one attack, on 30 July 1916, the King's lost 42 officers and 1,063 other ranks. On 8 August, three Battalions of the King's, as part of the 55th (West Lancashire) Division, took part in a further attack. After about 500 yards, the 5th King's was held up by heavy crossfire from enemy machine gun positions and was forced to dig in. The 8th Battalion advanced gallantly to Guillemont and succeeded in pushing into the village. Suddenly, however, they were attacked by enemy troops on their left flank and to the rear. They suffered enormous casualties with very few survivors. (The Liverpool Scottish were in action nearby, and for his valour in saving wounded men Noel Chavasse MC won his first Victoria Cross.) As usual, the advance had been preceded by heavy allied artillery fire, aimed at destroying the German positions. It later transpired that the Germans, having held Guillemont for many months, had dug themselves underground quarters which protected them from not only the allied bombardment but also troops, such as the 8th King's who as they advanced actually passed over the heads of the enemy. Once they had passed, the Germans came out of their shelters, taking up their former positions, often behind the advancing Allies. Three companies of the King's quickly over-ran enemy positions in Guillemont and moved forward. A fourth Company, following on behind into the village, was amazed to meet with strong resistance - the Germans had emerged from underground after the first three Companies had passed. Lt Col Goff, Commanding Officer of the 4th Company, was killed and nothing was ever heard of the other three companies.

On 3 September, what turned out to be the final assault on Guillemont was launched. The 12th Bn of the King's took part with 47th Brigade and the village was captured and held against German counter-attacks but not without difficulty and many casualties. They had to fight for every foot of ground as they advanced. This gave the German artillery time to move up and shell the advancing allies. In two days, the 12th Battalion lost 187 men of all ranks and the battle continued to rage, with counter-attacks on both sides.

On the night of 4/5 September, it was decided to relieve the 12th Bn as they had not rested for almost 72 hours. The 9th Borders were moved up into the line to replace them but had brought no Lewis guns with them. Instead of being relieved, Sergeant David Jones and his Lewis gunners were attached to the 9th Borders. While advancing to a forward position near Ginchy, the platoon to which they had been attached came under heavy machine gun fire, sustaining many losses, including the platoon officer who was killed. Sergeant Jones led forward the remaining members of the platoon, occupied their target position and held it for two days and two nights without food or water until they were relieved. On the second day they drove off three counter-attacks, inflicting heavy losses on the enemy. It was thanks to his coolness, resourcefulness and example that his men retained their confidence and held their position. For his actions, Jones was awarded the Victoria Cross. Michael Stedman, in his admirable guide to the Battle of Guillemont and others on the Somme, quotes at length an article which appeared in the *Liverpool Echo*:

> *'Sergeant Jones was the right man in the right place at the right time', was how a fellow non-commissioned officer of the Liverpool Regiment summed him up. 'We walked right into hell by the back door, and suffered terribly. All our officers bowled out. The men were like sheep without a shepherd. Things were all in a muddle. Nobody seemed to know what to do. Sergeant Jones sprang forward and gave orders. The men quickly recovered from their temporary dismay, and under his orders they resumed the rush on the enemy's position. The machine guns played hell with us, but the Sergeant led us straight to the goal. We carried the position with a rush, though we were greatly outnumbered. The enemy fled in panic and we lost no time in making ourselves at home in the position. All night long the enemy deluged us with shellfire and twice they attacked with great fury. They were determined to overwhelm us by sheer weight of numbers, but under the orders of Sergeant Jones we put our backs into it and drove off the Huns each time. We had neither food nor water and the circumstances were about as depressing as they could be, but Jones never despaired. He was so cheerful himself that everybody felt ashamed to be anything else. So we held on like grim death for two days. We smashed the enemy up every time they tried to overwhelm us. We had been given up for lost. Nobody ever expected to see us again. That we had come through the ordeal safe and with honour was entirely due to Sergeant Jones's handling of the men and nobody will begrudge him the honour he has won'.*

Another of his comrades said:

> *'He ought to be an officer. He led us with great skill, and completely baffled the foe at every turn. Nothing could dismay him. At times there*

was enough to make one's heart sink to the boots, but Sergeant Jones was as chirpy as could be and his cheeriness was infectious. We all felt sure that nothing could go wrong with us under his leadership and we were right'.

His citation in the *London Gazette* was equally impressive.

Totally unaware that he was to be awarded the Victoria Cross, Jones was now given an opportunity to go home on leave, but chose instead to return to the line with his comrades and was soon back in action. Perhaps inevitably, on 7 October 1916 at Bancourt on the Somme, he was killed in action. He died not knowing of his award, which was not announced until some two weeks after his death.

Thus ended, yet again, the short life of a remarkable man in the service of his country and fellow men. His grave is in Bancourt British Cemetery, Plot V.F.20.

At the date of his death, Elizabeth Jones was living at 203, Smithdown Lane, Edge Hill, Liverpool. (Family recollection is that her elder brother, Joseph, lived at 203 Smithdown Road.) Searching for information about his death, Jones's widow placed advertisements in the *Liverpool Echo*. Captain Norman Millican, an officer who had served with Jones responded on 2 November 1916 and, in addition to offering his condolences, added :

I was in the attack on 7 October and, as Senior Officer, became a little anxious as to what were the casualties. I remember asking my orderly at about 8.0pm, I think, and his first words were: 'Sergeant Jones, he that did so well at Ginchy, has been killed'. I felt very cut up as I had known him so long. Alas, many another brave man fell that day. But the Battalion, yes the whole Division, did wonderfully well. Accept my deepest sympathy for yourself in your irreparable loss of as brave and upright a man as one could wish for.

The writer, a patient at Endsleigh Palace Hospital in London, even apologised to Mrs Jones for his handwriting, explaining that 'my right hand is all bound up (not badly hurt), and I have to use my left hand'.

On 3 April 1917 a dual ceremony was held at Heyworth Street School, attended by pupils, crowds of local residents, members of the Education Committee and school management, the Headmaster and Mr Graham Reece, principal of Blake's Motor Company. Also present were Sergeant Jones's widow, his parents, the band of the 3rd Bn Royal Welsh Fusiliers, and a contingent of men from 9th and 12th Battalions of the King's (Liverpool) Regiment.

Inside the school, the Lord Mayor Councillor Max Muspratt, first unveiled a brass plaque, designed and engraved by John Ball. Then he unveiled a granite panel placed on the wall of the school, facing Heyworth Street. Speeches were made by the Headmaster and his predecessor and by the Lord Mayor, who said:

> *Sergeant Jones performed a deed of which the children of the school, the city and the Empire are proud. He has died for his country but the children now in the school have the opportunity of living for their country, with his inspiring example to stimulate them. He died that there should be a greater and better England, a happier and noble world.*

[My father was a pupil at Heyworth Street School at the time and told me of this ceremony, although he could not recall the name of David Jones. The brass plaque is now in the King's Regiment Museum, part of the Museum of Liverpool Life, while the granite stone is to be found in what was the public library at the corner of St Domingo Road and Mere Lane, Liverpool.] In 1961, Mr E.Kesslow, then living in Blackmoor Drive, West Derby, wrote to the *Liverpool Echo* to say that as a young teacher at Heyworth Street School he well remembered the day when the memorial stone was placed in a position high up the school wall: 'The granite was sent from Scotland where Mr Crosbie, the former head, was living in retirement'.

Jones's widow was presented with her husband's Victoria Cross by King George V, who asked her if she would wear it on her right breast. This she did on many occasions and although very proud of her husband's honour, was somewhat embarrassed when every serviceman she met duly saluted her! She eventually married William Woosey, a plumber, and they lived at 138 Portelet Road, Old Swan, Liverpool. She was unhappy when the King's Regiment was merged with the Manchester Regiment and on her death bequeathed David Jones's VC to his former employers Blakes, who had sent a representative from Liverpool to London to lay a wreath at the Cenotaph every year. This pilgrimage was started by his former employer, Stanley Blake Reece, himself a former Royal Flying Corps fighter pilot.

Postscript

Sid Lindsay's notes indicate that the medal was still held by Messrs Blakes, who considered it to be their proudest possession. Recently it became part of the King's Regiment Museum Collection at the Museum of Liverpool Life at the Albert Dock. An article in the *Liverpool Daily Post* on 26 August 1994 reported that the Managing Director of Blakes, Richard Coe, had presented the medal to the Museum, saying: 'We are delighted to know that in handing the VC over to the Museum of Liverpool Life far more Liverpool citizens will see it'.

David Jones VC plaque from Heyworth Street School

As a result of local publicity concerning the NCVCMA's plan to erect a memorial to Chavasse and the Liverpool-born VC holders, a relative of David Jones contacted us. Although she never knew him, David was her great-uncle and she kindly allowed us access to papers she had in her possession, including Captain Millican's letter. She also had a copy of a card sent by Major General W.Douglas Smith, Commanding Officer, 20th (Light) Division which reads: 'The Major General, 20th (Light) Division, has received a report of the gallant conduct of 14591 Sergt.W. [sic] Jones, 12th Kings Liverpool on 3rd September 1916 during the attack on Guillemont and he wishes to congratulate him on his fine behaviour', signed by Major General Smith himself.

*A*lbert White VC

Both *The Register of the Victoria Cross* (3rd Ed., 1997) and Sid Lindsay's research show that Albert White was born at 54, Lamb Street, Kirkdale, Liverpool, the son of Thomas and Susan (née Percival). His father was employed as a ship's carpenter, and after his education at Everton Terrace School, young Albert followed his father's example and took himself off to sea as a merchant seaman. The *Register* shows White as being born in 1896, while Sid's version is 1889. It is possible that both dates and the name of Albert's mother are incorrect. (See Postscript below.)

Albert was ashore when war broke out in August 1914, and on 23 October he enlisted in the Royal Army Medical Corps in Liverpool. On 1 June 1915 he transferred to the South Wales Borderers and was posted to the 2nd Battalion (which had been a component of a British-Japanese expeditionary force against the German occupied territory of Kiaochau and the port of Tsingtao, and part of the International Garrison at the city of Tientsin).

On 25 April 1915, the Battalion, now part of the 87th Brigade in the 29th Division, had landed on the open beaches at Cape Helles and attacked the well fortified Turkish positions. On 30 June Albert White arrived as one of the reinforcement troops. The horrors of the Gallipoli campaign are well documented. In August,1915, the Battalion took part in the assault on Suvla Bay and in October were back at Helles, having suffered terrible casualties. When they were evacuated and sent to Egypt in January 1916, they had lost 1600 officers and men in less than nine months.

They did not stay long in the comparative peace of Egypt, for in March 1916 they were moved to France with the rest of the 29th Division. After some retraining, they were in action in France at the Battle of the Somme; in July

Albert White was promoted to Sergeant. The Battalion was given the task of attacking the strongly defended German position at Beaumont Hamel. The 'Incomparable' 29th Division, the name they had given themselves after Gallipoli, were to attack via a natural declivity known as Y Ravine. It should be realised that the Germans had held Beaumont Hamel for a considerable time and had constructed strongpoints and dugouts in the natural chalky ground, affording themselves protection from the heaviest of the artillery attacks which the Allies could launch. The inevitable problems to be met by the 29th Division were awesome and they crumpled almost immediately in the face of intense machine gun fire. Headquarters, unaware of the carnage which had taken place, ordered that the attack be pressed forward, but this came to a halt because the way was clogged by dead and wounded. The attack was a total failure and Albert White's battalion lost 11 officers and 235 men killed or missing with four officers and 149 men wounded, from a total complement of 21 officers and 578 men. All had fallen in the first ten minutes after the attack began.

Today it is difficult to realise the true horrors of the Somme. The late Rose Coombs MBE, in her excellent work *Before Endeavours Fade* (Revised Edition, After the Battle 2006) described her feelings when she visited Beaumont some sixty years later:

> *And all around are the grass-covered trenches of the battlefield. All have been preserved as they were left in 1918 and, due to the fact that later battles did not alter them very much, it is possible to study and appreciate the actions fought here. Even on a fine summer's day, the park seems to have a definitely foreboding atmosphere and, after a thunderstorm I have smelt the awful stench of battle in the still, deep trenches. Nowhere else in my travels on the Western Front has the horror of war come nearer to me.*

Again, the 2nd Battalion had to be reformed but remained at the front and fought in a number of other important actions with great heroism. At about this time Albert White was offered a commission but after beginning preliminary training he felt obliged to withdraw for financial reasons. In April and May 1917, the Battalion saw action at Monchy-le-Preux during the Battle of Arras. It was during this battle in May 1917, that Sergeant White earned his Victoria Cross and sacrificed his own life.

On 19 May the Battalion was in a difficult position, having to 'make good' across a stretch of uneven ground dominated by enemy fire and without a vestige of cover. Sergeant White realised that example would count for much and demonstrated to his men an example of unflinching courage that was admired by all those who witnessed it. At one stage of the advance, White and his men were held up by the enemy and were wavering under withering fire. Without a moment's hesitation, White stepped forward and, with bullets whistling around him, dashed towards the next stage of the 'rush' to the enemy position. In the face of that example, his men could do only one thing - the once wavering line now raced forward and the gap in the line of their advance was closed up. It was in the final stage of the advance that Sergeant White was to prove his bravery in supreme fashion. He led the first group to try to rush towards the enemy. Before they had gone 50 yards, a concealed German machine gunner opened fire unexpectedly, threatening to halt the advance. Sergeant White realised the importance of maintaining forward impetus at this critical stage. At the same time, he would certainly have known the probable price to be paid to silence that machine gun. Absolutely fearlessly, he raced forward ahead of his company to try to capture the gun. He hurled himself at the enemy, shooting three and bayoneting a fourth, but as he closed on the gun he received a full charge and fell, riddled with bullets just yards from his target, and was killed.

Postscript by Bill Sergeant

Albert White's sacrifice of his own life in order that he might secure the success of the operations and the welfare of his comrades is yet another example of the supreme sacrifice so aptly stated on the headstone of Noel Chavasse - *'Greater love hath no man than this, that a man lay down his life for his friends'.* (It will also be inscribed on the proposed NCVCMA memorial to be erected in Liverpool, as described elsewhere in this book.) White has no known burial place, but he is remembered on Bay 6 of the Arras Memorial in the Faubourg-d'Amiens Cemetery in the western part of the town of Arras. His name appears in Brecon Cathedral alongside the names of the other four VC winners from the South Wales Borderers. Also in Brecon Cathedral is an illuminated Roll of Honour which records the names of almost 400 members of the diocese who served in the Great War, and which includes the following :

Year after year their life was a fine thing. They were in hell every day of their lives; and they endured it. They were in peril of death and worse than death, day after day and night after night; and they endured. They were exposed to all the nerve-shattering rage of artillery, artillery which rived the soil like an earthquake, which hurled the bodies of the dead into the air, and flung the bodies of the living into a deeper sepulchre; and they endured. They endured fire all these years, a manner of like utterly unnatural, and horrible beyond the expression of words. There has been nothing like this in the history of the world.

On 17 February 2006, I met with Mr George Thorn, whose late wife was a niece of Albert White. He remembers that for many years his mother-in-law had on display in her home a model of a Great War soldier, said to have been a model of Albert, kept in a glass dome on her sideboard. In front of the model was kept Albert's Victoria Cross. The dome, figure and Victoria Cross later went missing. Mr Thorn gave me the original of a letter dated 28 July 1917, signed by George V in which the King says:

It is a matter of sincere regret to me that the death of No.3/24866 Serjeant Albert White, 2nd Battalion, South Wales Borderers, deprived me of the pride of personally conferring upon him the Victoria Cross, the greatest of all rewards for valour and devotion to duty.

This letter was addressed to Mr Thomas White (Albert's father), 58 Lamb Street, Kirkdale, Liverpool. Sid Lindsay had given 54 Lamb Street as Albert's place of birth, and it is entirely possible that the family moved from 54 to 58 Lamb Street, a common practice in those days when private landlords might own several houses in one street. With this letter is another, pre-printed and with a facsimile signature, 'Milner, Secretary of State for War' which says:

The King commands me to assure you of the true sympathy of His Majesty and The Queen in your sorrow. He whose loss you mourn died in the noblest of causes. His Country will be ever grateful to him for the sacrifice he has made for Freedom and Justice.

As Alfred, 1st Viscount Milner, was not appointed to the position of Secretary of State for War until 19 April 1918, this letter, although undated, obviously postdates that from George V and is the standard letter sent to the families of those killed in the War.

Courtesy of the White family

With regard to Albert's date of birth, the 1891 Census shows Thomas and Eliza A White, with their children Thomas (b.1886), Robert (b.1888) and Elias (b.1889) living in Gillard Street, Kirkdale, and describes Thomas Senior (Albert's father) as a railway porter born in Scotland. The 1901 Census has them living at 124 Arlington Street, Kirkdale, with young Thomas, now 15 years old, shown as a biscuit maker. There are two more children in the family now - Albert, born 1892, and Jessie, born 1899. Eliza is now shown as Elizabeth. Surviving members of the family do recall a connection with Arlington Street, which tends to suggest that Albert's parents were Thomas and Elizabeth; some notes given to me by the Victoria Cross and George Cross Association state that Albert had a sister, Jessie White. A search of local records show that a Susan Percival married a *James* White in early 1894, by which time all of Albert's brothers and his sister had already been born. In early 1883, *Thomas* White married Eliza Ann Falls. I have also traced a birth record for an Albert White, showing that he was born on 1 December 1892, the son of Thomas and Eliza Ann White née Falls, at 62 Teulon Street, Kirkdale, Liverpool. I am satisfied that this is Albert White VC.

The difficulty I have experienced not only with Albert but with others amongst our 'Liverpool heroes' is that incorrect information tends to become widely accepted and then appears in what one would normally expect to be 'official' records. For example, the Victoria Cross and George Cross Association's notes repeat Sid's belief that Albert was the son of Thomas and Susan née Percival. They do, however, suggest that he was born c1892 and include a note to the effect that he had a sister called Jessie. All of this, other than his mother's name, coincides with the family who lived in Arlington Street. At some time the family moved to Lamb Street, where Thomas White senior was still living in 1917.

$\mathcal{R}$onald Neil Stuart VC DSO

Ronald Neil Stuart was born on 26 August 1886 at 31 Kelvin Grove, Toxteth Park, Liverpool, the son of Captain Neil Stuart and his wife, Mary (née Banks). His father had been born on Prince Edward Island, Canada, and his mother was born in Liverpool. A grandson of Ronald, Mr Craig Buchanan, says that family recollection is that Mary Banks lived at the Kelvin Grove address with her sister, Sarah, where they ran a dressmaking business. Next door at No. 33 lived Captain David Sutherland, a friend of Sarah. One day Captain Sutherland announced that he was bringing home with him to dine a handsome husband for Sarah to marry. The handsome man was Neil Stuart who married Mary instead of Sarah! The Stuart family had a long seafaring history and Neil is reputed to have run off to sea when only 14 years of age and to have sailed during the American Civil War. He was at one time the captain of a paddle steamer on the Mississippi and sailed clippers between Canada, the United Kingdom and Australia.

Ronald was the youngest child of six, and the only boy. Craig Buchanan quotes family recollections stating that none of the five girls married. The eldest, Mary Catharine, born in Montreal in 1876 (it is thought that her mother was probably on a voyage with her husband) lived until 1976. He describes her as a 'slave to her mother...brought up to be innocent'. The second daughter, Ethel Maud, born in Liverpool and who died 1949, he describes as 'tall, gaunt, the brightest of that generation', and said to have been the headmistress of 'the senior Jewish school in Liverpool'. She died of tuberculosis in the 1930s. The third daughter, Lillian Hannah, born in 1882 in Liverpool, was always referred to in whispers by her sisters as Poor Lillian – she died aged 45 years in the Lancaster County Mental Hospital. Next came Amy Sarah, who was born in Liverpool and died in 1965; she was said by the family to have been 'red-haired, malicious, vindictive, with a ferocious temper and absolutely fearless'. Amy was a qualified nurse and as a member of Queen Alexandra's Royal Army Nursing Corps (QARANC), spent much of the Great War on Malta, nursing casualties from Gallipoli, and later in France at a Casualty Clearing Station. She was awarded an 'ARRC', (Associate of the Royal Red Cross), which is described as being the equivalent of a Distinguished Service Cross or Military Cross. The fifth daughter, Agnes, was born in Liverpool and died in 1954; she was also a nurse, specialising in problem new babies but, in the words of Craig, only 'upper class' babies! The 1881 Census shows Mary Stuart with her three daughters, Mary Catherine, Ethel Maud and Lilian Hannah, together with a female servant, living at 40 Claribel Street, Liverpool. The 1901 Census has Mary, now a 53-year-old widow, living at 31 Kelvin Grove with Mary, Ethel, Lilian, Amy, Agnes and Ronald Neil, aged 14 years.

Family gossip suggests that at some stage, Captain Neil Stuart, Ronald's father, 'swallowed the anchor' in Liverpool, ie gave up the sea, and opened a grocery shop in Prescot Road. He did not settle at this, but as he was about to return to sea, he became ill and died.

Ronald Neil Stuart was educated at Liverpool Collegiate School, Shaw Street, Liverpool and in 1902, at the age of 15 years, went off to sea as an apprentice in the iron barque *Kirkhill*, owned by Joseph Steel & Company, 17 Water Street, Liverpool. She was built in 1891 and weighed 1540 tons. In only the third year of Ronald's apprenticeship, *Kirkhill* was wrecked off the Falkland Islands, but he survived unscathed. On completion of his training, he joined the Allan Line, which at that time was the principal carrier between the United Kingdom and Canada and in 1908 had 18 liners crossing the Atlantic. The company had been in collaboration with the Canadian Pacific Railway Company (CPR) for some time, chartering each others' vessels, and in 1915, when CPR had been granted permission to operate its railways and shipping line separately, they announced that they had also acquired the Allan Line. Ronald Neil Stuart stayed with them.

In early 1914, he joined the Royal Naval Reserve as a probationer sub-lieutenant and was confirmed in that rank in May 1915. He served in several ships but was eventually selected for special service in 'Q' ships, being made 1st Lieutenant to Gordon Campbell, RN (later awarded a Victoria Cross himself and a life-long friend of the Stuart family). 'Q' ships looked like merchant ships but carried concealed armaments. Their purpose was to combat attack from

German submarines by giving the appearance of an unarmed vessel, luring the submarine to the surface and then blasting it out of the water. One often-used ploy was to put a 'panic party' of apparently unarmed civilian passengers into a lifeboat to support the pretence. One such ship, a former collier named *Loderer*, was converted to a Q ship at Devonport and renamed *Farnborough*. In March 1916 Campbell and Stuart were aboard her when they sighted a German submarine which discharged a torpedo at the *Farnborough* but missed her. They went into their well-rehearsed act and the submarine (U68) closed in and surfaced. As she did so, she was hit by *Farnborough's* guns and then finished off with depth charges.

A year later, in March 1917, they got their next kill. Spotting a torpedo tracking towards them, Campbell turned the *Farnborough* to ensure that they were hit astern. They sent off a 'panic party' and the submarine broke surface some 300 yards away. Campbell could see that the conning tower was open and the U-Boat Commander was on the bridge but had to wait for it to pass on the beam before he was able to bring his concealed guns to bear. The submarine came to within 100 yards before *Farnborough's* gunners opened fire at point blank range, sending over 40 shells into the U-Boat, which sank with only two survivors. *Farnborough* herself had suffered torpedo damage and began to settle in the water but was taken into tow by the Royal Navy destroyer HMS *Narwhal* and sloop HMS *Buttercup* and successfully beached. She was later repaired and remained in peacetime service until 1926 as the *Holypark*.

For this action, Gordon Campbell was awarded the Victoria Cross and Stuart received the Distinguished Service Order.

Their next ship, another Q ship, was the converted collier *Pargust*. As a result of the *Farnborough's* experiences, the *Pargust* was significantly more heavily-armed, with a 4" gun and four 12-pounders, two 14" torpedo tubes and depth charge facilities. She was commissioned on 28 March 1917 and set off into the Atlantic, virtually hoping to be torpedoed. At 8.00am on 7 June, she got her wish and was hit to starboard, the torpedo having been fired at close range, leaving the crew no chance to take avoiding action. Once again, a 'panic party' fled the ship by lifeboat and the submarine's periscope was seen circling the stricken *Pargust*. The 'panic party' turned as if to re-board their vessel and the U-Boat commander, taking the bait, surfaced but too far astern to be a target. He turned to the starboard side of the *Pargust* and came up onto the bridge of the submarine. Seizing their opportunity, Campbell ordered his hidden gunners to open fire and shells bombarded the U-Boat. Unable to submerge, she tried vainly to escape on the surface but exploded a short distance away. Once again there were only two survivors and it was later learned that they were from *UC29*, a mine-laying submarine which had been terrorising the Atlantic shipping lanes off the coast of Ireland.

George V had a personal interest in the deeds of Q ships, whose operations could only be described as 'suicidal in the service of the nation', and he indicated that the whole crew should be considered for the Victoria Cross. Under Rule 13 of the Royal Warrant of 1856, the ship's company held a ballot for one officer and one seaman to receive the award as representatives of the ship, electing Lt Ronald Neil Stuart DSO and AB William Williams DSM. Stuart's VC was the first ever awarded to an Anglo-Canadian serving with the Imperial Forces. At the time, as in the case of Campbell a year earlier, the citation made no reference to the full circumstances except to state that it had been earned in action against enemy submarines. Campbell received a Bar to his DSO and was promoted to Captain, while the *Pargust* was towed to Plymouth and paid off.

With one notable exception, the same crew as that originally mustered under Campbell joined him on his next Q ship, the *Dunraven*. The exception was Ronald Neil Stuart VC, who was given command of his own Q ship, the *Tamarisk*. While in this post, Stuart was to receive high recognition from the United States Government. On 15 October 1917, the US destroyer *Cassin* had her stern blown off by a German torpedo. One seaman was killed, five were wounded and the vessel could not be steered. With great difficulty in heavy seas and at considerable risk from another attack, Stuart managed to get a line aboard the *Cassin* and successfully towed her into port. For his efforts, he was awarded the United States Navy Cross. In 1918, he was appointed Lt Commander RNR and is believed to have been awarded the Croix de Guerre with Palms, although Craig Buchanan says the family has no knowledge of such an award being made.

After the war, Ronald Neil Stuart VC kept on with his dual career with the Royal Naval Reserve and the Canadian Pacific. On Saturday 19 July 1924, King George V accompanied by Queen Mary visited Liverpool for the consecration of the Anglican Cathedral, and in the afternoon in Wavertree Playground, Liverpool, reviewed the 55th West Lancashire Territorial Division. Lt Commander Stuart, VC RNR, was one of nine VC holders presented to the King. Also present was Cyril Edward Gourley VC, another of the 16 brave men featured in this book. Stuart trained regularly with the RNR, being promoted to full Commander in June 1928 and the following year was awarded the Reserve Officer's Decoration. On 1 July 1935 he was promoted Captain RNR and was elected President of the RNR Officers Club. By virtue of a special Ensign Warrant of 14 May 1927, he was authorised to fly the Blue Ensign on any ship under his command.

His service with the Canadian Pacific was equally meritorious; he was appointed Staff Captain on the liner *Empress of France* from 1924 to 1926, when he became Captain of the *Minnedosa*, a 14,000 ton liner which had been used for troop transportation for a short time in 1918. He was Captain of the new *Duchess of York*, whose maiden voyage was out of Liverpool on 22 March 1929, and in November of that year brought a party of Canadian Victoria Cross holders across to attend the Victoria Cross Dinner at the Guildhall, London. In 1934, he became Captain of the 42,000 ton *Empress of Britain* and was appointed Commodore of the Canadian Pacific fleet, a position he held until 1936, when he gave up his command to become General Superintendent in Montreal. In 1938, he was appointed General Manager in London. He suffered a great blow in 1940 when the *Empress of Britain* was torpedoed in the North Atlantic by a German U-boat (U32). In 1941 he became Naval Aide de Camp to King George V, and in 1951 he retired.

Stuart knew at first hand the rigours of being at sea in all kinds of vessels and all kinds of conditions. He was a hard taskmaster who did not suffer fools gladly. There is a story that when the first CPR ship was sunk in 1940, an Irishman sent a postcard to the Company saying that he had found the name-board of the sunken ship, *Beaverburn*, and was claiming the reward of £1 which he believed to be due to him. The Company's General Manager (R.N.Stuart) made a written comment on the card that if a stamped, self-addressed envelope had not been received with this enquiry no reply should be sent!

In July 1919, he had married Evelyn Wright, the daughter of W.Wright of West Derby, at St Clement's Church, Dove Street, Toxteth, Liverpool. They had three sons and two daughters. Two sons served in the Navy during the Second World War - one in the Royal Navy and the other in the Canadian Navy. One, also named Ronald Neil, was awarded a Distinguished Service Cross. Ronald's wife died in 1930 or 1931, and Craig Buchanan's website notes: 'After his wife died, he put the children in the hands of his sisters-in-law which was understandable but was not a happy decision'. Upon his retirement, he went to live with his sisters at Beryl Lodge, Charing in Kent, where he died on 8 February 1954, aged 67 years. He is buried in Charing Cemetery, and his medals are on display in the National Maritime Museum, Greenwich. There is a Stuart Road, named after him, in Lee on Solent, Hampshire.

*W*illiam Ratcliffe VC MM

William Ratcliffe was born on 18 February 1884, at 38 Newhall Street, Liverpool, the son of William and Mary Ann (née Kelly). At the time, his father was employed as a carter by one of the many haulage firms in the city. [Records of his early life had been difficult to locate until very recently when, following the launch of the NCVCMA project, members of his family made contact with the Association. It is now clear that he attended St Vincent's School in the Dingle. Newhall Street still exists, in the vicinity of Jamaica Street near Queen's Dock, but the houses have been demolished.]

Upon leaving school, William began work on the docks but left at the age of 16 when he enlisted in the South Lancashire Regiment and eventually took part in the South African War. His army records suggest that he might have provided a false date of birth when enlisting. He signed on for 12 years and on completing his service was discharged, returning to work on the Liverpool docks. Immediately upon the outbreak of war on 4 August 1914 he rejoined the South Lancashire Regiment and soon found himself in France, where he saw action in several of the early battles. He earned a reputation for having absolutely no regard for his own safety whenever he went into action. His daring impatience, it seemed, led to his somewhat charmed life.

In April, 1917, he was in action at Messines Ridge, some six miles south of Ypres and the scene of much bloody fighting. His company were suffering heavy casualties at the hands of well-positioned enemy snipers, when William Ratcliffe decided to do some sniping of his own and quickly accounted for seven German marksmen. For this, he was awarded the Military Medal. The General who pinned the medal upon his chest in France jokingly remarked on learning of Ratcliffe's reputation: 'We shall have you getting the other one next', meaning the Victoria Cross.

Two months later, on 12 June, two days before the Battle of Messines began, the South Lancashire Regiment was given the objective of capturing the Ferme de la Croix to secure the northern bank of the River Douve. The attack started on 14 June and the allied supporting artillery, instead of maintaining a creeping barrage as agreed, put down a curtain of fire beyond their objective. Ratcliffe's and other companies were then obliged to hurry onto the enemy positions beyond the barrage. As it happened, this allied misunderstanding seemed to catch the Germans by surprise and the Battalion advanced on their lines. There were, however, a number of machine gun nests which had escaped the barrage and these began to create havoc among the allied troops. It was at this point that Pte William Ratcliffe earned the Victoria Cross as his General had forecast. In the words of the 75th Infantry Brigade Commander:

> *Private Ratcliffe was an old soldier with the South African War Medal. He was a stretcher-bearer and had done distinguished service on the Somme, where he had earned his Military Medal. In this attack, he was following his platoon and, on reaching the first objective saw a Boche machine gun in action, which had not been mopped up and was firing into the flank and rear of his comrades. He at once dropped his stretcher and, seizing a dead man's rifle, went straight for the machine gun and bayoneted the German officer and five of his crew. He then picked up the machine gun and some ammunition and ran after his company, and when they had reached their final objective, he brought the gun into action against the enemy. He then went back, retrieved his stretcher and spent the rest of the night bringing in the wounded through a heavy barrage. Never was the spirit and gallant devotion more exemplified than by this fine old soldier.*

At this time, Ratcliffe was 33 years of age, not 'old' in terms of human life, but certainly 'old' compared with his youthful comrades, especially when so many men much younger than himself were falling about him, and in terms of military experience.

He received his Victoria Cross from HM King George V in October 1917, and then came to Liverpool where, on 13 October, he attended a dinner and presentation given in his honour by the National Union of Dock Labourers. Lord Derby, who was also present, responded to the toast by saying that he was pleased that a proposed monetary gift to Ratcliffe was not to take place that evening, as it was an offence to reward a soldier with money for doing his duty.

He was, however, very happy to agree to such a presentation being made when Ratcliffe returned to civilian life. He then announced that he would do everything in his power to grant extra leave to Pte Ratcliffe to enable him to get a Bar to his Cross by getting married - this was greeted by much laughter.

In the event, Bill Ratcliffe did not marry, but lived with his sister and her family in Brindley Street, between Grafton Street and Caryl Street, parallel to Parliament Street. He later moved to 29a, St Oswald's Gardens, Old Swan, Liverpool, where he was looked after by his niece and great-niece. After his discharge, he returned to work on the docks. He died on 26 March, 1963 and after Requiem Mass at St Oswald's Church, was buried in Allerton Cemetery, in the grave of his niece, Sarah Humes, and her husband, John Walsh, who both predeceased him. Their grave is No 274 in plot RC19.

In the Branch Office of the Transport and General Workers Union, then situated in St James Place, South Liverpool, there used to be a stone tablet, purchased by the Branch members, to commemorate Bill Ratcliffe's great courage. The Branch was later closed down and the tablet has been lost. A portrait of Ratcliffe was said to have hung in the old Branch office, but that too is missing. Shortly after the TGWU office was vacated and demolished, there was a report in a local newspaper that a passer-by had found the tablet, damaged, in a rubbish skip, and efforts are being made to discover whether or not this is true. If the tablet and portrait are located, connections with Liverpool's 'Docker VC' will be renewed.

Postscript

As a result of the launch of the NCVCMA Project in November 2005, relatives of three of our local VC winners have made contact. These included Mrs Josephine Gornall, the granddaughter of William Ratcliffe's older sister, Mary Jane, who was able to confirm and correct information about William Ratcliffe's family. She explained that her grandmother was the second eldest in a family of 5 children born to William and Mary Anne: the oldest was Sarah, then came Mary Jane, Alice, Peter and finally William Ratcliffe. Mrs Gornall's mother apparently was divorced from her husband – in those days and in such a Catholic environment this was not something to be encouraged. She was to some extent ostracised by the rest of the family. Mrs Gornall consequently did not get to know her 'Uncle Bill' particularly well, but her mother often spoke of him. Mrs Gornall recalls being taken to the cinema in the 1960s by her mother, when some old Pathé news footage was shown, of Bill Ratcliffe VC being given a civic reception in Liverpool in 1917. She recalls that her mother pointed out several of the family featured in the newsreel. She also kept several newspaper articles, published in the *Liverpool Echo*, relating to her Great Uncle Bill. On 20 June 1956, the *Echo* reported that Bill Ratcliffe, 'Liverpool's second oldest living holder of the Victoria Cross' was that day parading in Hyde Park before Queen Elizabeth and the Duke of Edinburgh, as part of the celebration of the centenary of the medal's institution by Queen Victoria. He was accompanied by his niece (Margaret Walsh) and wore a suit which had been given to him by a local gent's outfitter as Bill did not possess a decent suit - the suit was said to have cost fifteen guineas. 'And very smart it is too', said Bill, who felt 'a real toff with a new black trilby, new shoes and new gloves as well'. (The oldest living Liverpool recipient of the VC at the time was Donald Farmer, then 78 years old and living in Greenhill Road, Liverpool, who also attended the celebrations. Donald Dickson Farmer VC was in fact born in Roxburghshire, Scotland, but after service with the Royal Scots Regiment was promoted in 1909 to Colour Sergeant Instructor to the 10th (Scottish) Battalion of the King's (Liverpool) Regiment and on discharge settled here in Liverpool. His story will feature in a later volume.) Mrs Noreen Hill, a relative, has recently confirmed that the suit was provided by the Victoria Cross Association.

William Ratcliffe medal group
Photo W. Sergeant

On 6 April 1963 the *Liverpool Echo* reported on his funeral, which was attended by a 'quiet little group', which 'made a strange contrast to the cheering thousands who lined the streets on August 30, 1917 to hail that same modest man. But memories fade and the well-nigh unbelievable gallantry which, in World War One, had earned Private Bill Ratcliffe the Victoria Cross and the Military Medal, had been forgotten long ago, except by the few. On his homecoming for a few days leave after he had been awarded the VC in 1917, the whole of Liverpool turned out to greet him'.

In February 1991, the *Echo* reported on Sid Lindsay's presentation to the Lord Mayor of Liverpool of a framed 'Roll of Honour' (currently still displayed in Liverpool Town Hall) featuring the names of 14 Liverpool-born VC holders, including Ratcliffe. Mrs N.Dwyer of West Derby wrote in to say that she recalled seeing his victorious homecoming some 74 years earlier, and as a little girl with her mother, recalled 'the cheers and clapping when he arrived in a horse-drawn carriage which I suppose was the Lord Mayor's coach'. She also clarified a point which Sid Lindsay had been unable to resolve: she explained that she had attended St Vincent's School, Norfolk Street, off Park Lane. 'It was a great honour for the school as William Ratcliffe had been a pupil there and a celebration was planned for him. A raised platform was built in the playground and all the local dignitaries, our clergy and teachers were present. The pupils were assembled and we sang this song:

> *Billy, Billy Ratcliffe, you are a great brave-hearted man,*
> *A credit to your country and all your native land.*
> *May your arm be ever steady and your aim be ever true,*
> *God Bless you, Billy Ratcliffe, here's your country's love to you.*

Another great-niece, Mrs Noreen Hill, also made contact. She is the daughter of Margaret Walsh née Humes and, with her mother, had escorted Ratcliffe to London in 1956. Mrs Hill suggested that Peter Ratcliffe, William's older brother, was drowned when the *Lusitania* went down in 1915, and the family story was that when he won one of his medals, Bill Ratcliffe, in response to a request for volunteers for a mission, said that the Germans had robbed him of his brother and he had nothing more to lose – this might explain his reputation for being fearless. Reference to the *Lusitania* crew list found that Peter Ratcliffe was a fireman whose body was never recovered. Mrs Hill also believed that the family had lived elsewhere in the Dingle area before Brindley Street. The 1881 Census revealed an entry showing William and Mary A.Ratcliffe, with their three children - Sarah aged 5 years, Peter aged 3 years and Mary Jane aged 8 months - living at Blundell Street, 7 Court 5 House. Such an inauspicious beginning for such a valiant man!

Mrs Hill further confirmed, through a copy of his birth certificate in her possession, that William Ratcliffe was born on 18 February 1884. Various sources had previously shown some confusion about this date. She was also able to provide some details about an accident on the docks, which occurred before 1947. Two one-ton bags of castor seeds fell on him, causing neck, pelvis and spinal injuries and leaving him stone deaf. He was not covered by insurance, received no lump sum compensation but did have a pension of £2 per week for life. Family stories have it that after the accident, Billy was pronounced dead and taken to the mortuary, where he suddenly woke up!

As he grew older, he took to drinking heavily and in 1963, on the way to his local public house in Old Swan, he fell and was taken to hospital by ambulance. He was unable to tell the hospital staff who he was and was only located and identified when Noreen and her mother made their own enquiries as he had failed to return home. He died on 26 March 1963, in hospital. Mrs Hill contacted the South Lancashire Regiment and was assisted with the funeral arrangements by Major Ryan. Ratcliffe's funeral, which was also attended by other military personnel, including a Colonel, was reported in the local press, including the *Catholic Pictorial*.

Mrs Hill also showed me a booklet containing the names of all the VC holders who attended the Hyde Park Centenary Celebrations in 1956. Of these, the following, all with Liverpool or Merseyside connections, were present: Marcus Beak, VC DSO MC; Joe Counter; Donald Farmer; Ian Fraser; Cyril Gourley (shown as G.E.Gourlay); Joseph Lister; Arthur Procter; and Joe Tombs. Also there, in a contingent of Canadian VC holders, were Cecil Kinross and Major Harry Mullin. Both earned their medals at Passchendaele at the same time as Hugh McKenzie VC (see Chapter 16). In fact, Mullin was in the same attack which saw McKenzie lose his life.

At the same time, on display in the Centenary Exhibition in Marlborough House, were a photograph of John Kirk; the VC and medals of Charles Anderson; a group photograph of Harry Hampton, William Heaton and Henry Knight - currently on display in the King's Regiment Museum, Liverpool; the VC, medals and a photograph of Arthur Richardson; colour print and ship's bell from HMS *Clyde*, commanded by Edward Unwin; group photograph of Joseph Tombs, Joseph Counter and Arthur Procter; photograph of Gabriel Coury; steel helmet belonging to Thomas Alfred Jones; portrait, VC and Bar of Noel Chavasse; VC, cap, goggles belonging to Thomas Mottershead; VC and medals of John Sinton; and a German machine gun captured by Billy Ratcliffe. All of those named, although possibly not mentioned in this booklet, have Merseyside connections and will feature in this series.

Cyril Edward Gourley
VC MM

Cyril Edward Gourley was born on 19 January 1893 at 6, Victoria Park, Wavertree, Liverpool 15. He was the son of Galbraith and Martha Anne ('Cissie'). Galbraith, who was a native of Ireland, and his brother were partners in the firm of Gourley Brothers, prominent wholesale provision merchants with an office in Dove Street, Liverpool 8 and branches in Lawrence Road and Smithdown Road in Liverpool and Brighton Street, Seacombe. In 1899, the family moved from Wavertree to live at 23, North Road, West Kirby, Wirral and the 1901 Census shows Galbraith and Martha living at this address with their six children, all under the age of 10 years. That year they moved to 39 Westbourne Road, West Kirby, and in 1925 moved to 'Hill Close' School Lane, off Column Road, West Kirby. Young Cyril, the second born of their five boys, was educated at Caldy Grange Grammar School, where he distinguished himself by winning an Edward Rathbone Scholarship before going on to Liverpool University. In 1913, he became the first to take the Final Examination for the new degree of Bachelor of Commercial Sciences, gaining distinctions in French, Economics and Commerce.

On leaving university, Cyril took employment with the well-known Liverpool shipping and merchant firm of Alfred Holt & Company, owners of the Blue Funnel Shipping Line. On 19 May 1914, he joined the Territorial Army, a common practice in shipping offices, as a private in the 4th West Lancashire Howitzer Brigade, Royal Field Artillery, based at 'The Grange' on the corner of Edge Lane and Botanic Road. There were two batteries here, known as the 7th and the 8th.

The Brigade was mobilised on 4 August 1914 and went first to the Sevenoaks area and then Canterbury, Kent. On 28 September 1915 they embarked for France with their horses and guns, on two ships - one belonging to the Elder Dempster Line and the other being the Isle of Man steamer *Mona's Queen*. They moved into the line in the Kemmel area, south of Ypres, as part of the 55th West Lancs Division and were involved in sporadic action. In January 1916 they moved to Pont-Rémy, between Abbeville and Amiens, and here the composition of the batteries was changed so that the howitzer brigades ceased to exist as such. There was now to be one howitzer battery and three 18-pounder batteries to each group. The old 7th and 8th batteries became D/276 and D/275 but here they will be referred to by their original designations. Just before these changes were fully completed, the two batteries moved to positions in the Crinchon Valley, six miles south-west of Arras, to reinforce the defence of Verdun.

On 20 July 1916 they began moving to positions on the Somme and were deployed near the infamous village of Guillemont, the scene already of so much fierce fighting and bloodshed and located in the romantic sounding French Province of Picardy. [The Battle of the Somme started on 1 July 1916 and fighting in the area continued until virtually the end of the war in 1918. Guillemont was the scene of some of the most bitter warfare, from July until September 1916, during which the village was reduced to a heap of ruins and the Kings Regiment alone sustained almost 3000 casualties of all ranks.] Gourley and his comrades saw frequent action in the Guillemont area, and in late September moved back to the Ypres area where they were soon in action again. Although throughout the winter the infantry were restricted to relatively minor skirmishes, the artillery were regularly subjected to enemy barrages.

On 1 June 1917 the batteries became part of the massed 2,233 pieces of artillery which rained shells on the enemy for almost a week preceding the attack by the Allies on the Messines Ridge. Here Sgt Cyril Gourley was awarded the Military Medal. His battery was shelling the enemy and had stockpiled a considerable amount of ammunition, when an enemy shell dropped amongst them, setting fire to the camouflage covering the guns and the ammunition, putting the ammunition dump at considerable risk. There is no doubt that if it had exploded, there would have been many casualties. Sgt Gourley promptly extinguished the fire and saved the situation.

In the third week of November, the batteries moved off to take part in the first Battle of Cambrai. This battle started on 20 November 1917, when two of 3rd

Army's Corps, supported by 378 tanks (the first time the Allies used fighting tanks) and 1000 guns quickly captured 7500 enemy soldiers and 120 of their guns. On 30 November, however, the Germans launched a counter-attack. Gourley's 7th Battery took up their position at Little Priel Farm, south-east of Epehy and some ten miles north-west of St Quentin. The battery opened fire at about 7.00 am and quickly found themselves under heavy enemy fire. One of the Section Officers was seriously wounded by shrapnel and the Battery Commander, Major J.Hudson MC, having no other officer available, sent Sgt Gourley MM to take charge. The enemy maintained their barrage and it was seen that their infantry, in large numbers, was moving in close to the Allied forward positions in an attempt to breach the lines. One of the British guns was completely out of action and it was now that Cyril Gourley earned his Victoria Cross.

The citation in the *London Gazette* of 13 February 1918 states:

> *For most conspicuous bravery when in command of a company of howitzers. Though the enemy advanced in force, getting within 400 yards in front, between 300 and 400 yards to one flank and with some snipers to the rear, Sergeant Gourley managed to keep one gun in action practically throughout the day. Though frequently driven off he always returned carrying ammunition, laying and firing the gun himself, taking first one and then another of the detachment to assist him. When the enemy approached, he pulled his gun out of the pit and engaged a machine gun at 500 yards, knocking it out with a direct hit. All day he held the enemy in check, firing with open sights on enemy parties in full view at 300 to 800 yards, and thereby saved his guns which were withdrawn at nightfall.*

On 5 January 1918, he was commissioned as 2nd Lt in the Royal Field Artillery. He remained with the now famous 55th Division until it was disbanded in the spring of 1919, in Brussels. He was appointed Acting Captain on 19 May 1919 and came home to be demobilised the following month. It is interesting to note that although holding a commissioned rank at the time of his investiture, he attended in his sergeant's uniform, which he also wore for his visit to Liverpool when he was given a civic reception. It has been said that he was unable to obtain a commission in the earliest days of his service because of defective eyesight – perhaps this rejection still rankled and accounts for his reluctance to wear officer's dress for his investiture.

On leaving the army, he joined the firm of Lever Brothers in the export department, then known as the Marketing Advisory Service. He showed the same dedication as when he was a soldier, and it was largely due to his efforts that markets for Lever Brothers' products were developed in the Balkans, Central and South

America and the Mediterranean countries. He was a very quiet and courteous gentleman, ever ready to help others but shunning the adulation his great honour merited. He continued to work until his retirement in 1958, having moved south in 1952 to live with his mother and sister at Grayswood House, Grayswood, near Haslemere, Surrey. For the next 23 years, he followed a life of modest activity, restoring his beautiful home and gardens and taking an interest in the associated farmlands. He did not marry.

Gourley died peacefully in his sleep in 1982 at the age of 89 years. His body was brought back to West Kirby to be buried with his parents in Grange Cemetery. After the award of his Victoria Cross, the C.E.Gourley VC Endowment had been founded in his honour through a Trust Deed dated 30 September 1919, by a committee responsible to the Hoylake and West Kirby Urban District Council. The sum of £1,500 was subscribed to provide a scholarship of £30 per year for Liverpool University.

The Gourley Brothers firm has been taken over but continues to use the name. The shops have long disappeared. 'Hill Close', the West Kirby home of the Gourleys for many years, became known as 'Gourley's Grange'', Gourley's Lane, in his honour. It is now scheduled for demolition. There is a Gourley Road, in Liverpool, apparently named after him.

In the Second World War Cyril Gourley, like so many others, did his bit as a firewatcher during the many air raids on Merseyside.

The *Liverpool Echo* dated 6 March 1918 included an assessment of his deeds and character. Under the headline 'BASHFUL HERO', it reported:

> *The V.C. who 'stuck to his guns all day' and kept the Germans at bay almost unaided, had an attack of nerves when he met his colleagues at the Liverpool University. Sergeant Cyril Gourley VC, MM had a particularly cordial welcome today. Some hundreds of students were in the liveliest form and the echoing cheers and a noisy rattle, if they had been pitched in a lower key, would have resembled an 'artillery' demonstration. Vice-Chancellor Dale, in one of his felicitous speeches, congratulated the modest hero on the honour he had gained and mentioned that five VCs had now been won by old graduates and undergraduates of the University. Shaking hands with his parents and sister, who were witnesses of the interesting scene, he also tendered his heartiest congratulations to them. Sergeant Gourley, flushed and bashful, drew the line at making a speech. In comparison with that, the ordeal of battle was a triviality. So the Vice Chancellor, pleading that time was precious, let the students once more give vent to their feelings as only students can and hastened away with him to see the Lord Mayor.*

On 19 July 1924, like Ronald Neil Stuart VC, Cyril Gourley was among the nine VC holders presented to King George V at Wavertree Playground, Liverpool. He was one of those who actually spoke to the King. There are memorials to Gourley in Grayswood College, Chiddingfold, Surrey and at West Kirby, Wirral.

Presentation of the Victoria Cross certificate by the late Sid Lindsay to the Lord Mayor, Cllr. Dorothy Gavin, Liverpool Town Hall.

*H*ugh McDonald McKenzie
VC, DCM
by
Bill Sergeant

Introduction

Hugh McDonald McKenzie came to our notice after Sid Lindsay's death and does not feature in the framed certificate which Sid created and which is displayed in Liverpool Town Hall (opposite page). We are taking steps to rectify this omission. Although born in Liverpool, McKenzie lived his early life in Scotland before emigrating to Canada. He was with a Canadian Regiment in the First World War when awarded his Victoria Cross. I am grateful to the archivist of the Princess Patricia's Canadian Light Infantry Museum, who kindly provided me with much biographical detail, and to John Mulholland who supplied me with other information.

* * *

Hugh McDonald McKenzie was born on 5 December 1885 in Liverpool, the son of James McKenzie and Jane McDonald McKenzie. His mother was brought up in Inverness, Scotland and her family lived at Blackpark of Muirtown, her father having been an Elder of the Free North Church during the ministries of Dr George McKay and the Reverend Murdo MacKenzie. Hugh's father, James, was a Highlander and brought up in the Coupar Angus District of Scotland. He was a marine engineer and during his absences at sea his wife and family lived in Inverness. James was originally a sugar boiler in a confectionery factory but because he could not find employment he joined the Merchant Navy. He and Jane had four sons and three daughters.

During the time that James McKenzie was sailing out of Liverpool, his family moved to the city and Hugh was born. In 1887 when he was only two years old, his father was lost at sea and the family moved back to Inverness. Hugh attended Leachkin School and was subsequently employed by Mr Robert Thompson at Kinmylies, and later entered the service of the Highland Railway as a cleaner. In about 1905, Mrs McKenzie and her family left Inverness to live in Dundee, but always spent their annual holidays in Inverness. (For years, Dundee claimed that Hugh went to school there, but research suggests that they were confusing him with another Hugh McKenzie, born in Dundee on 29 December 1885.)

In Dundee, Hugh took up employment with Messrs Watson & Sons of Seagate and also with the Caledonian Railway Company as a carter, before he married and moved to Canada. Described as a young man of splendid physique, Hugh was one of the founders of the Dundee amateur boxing and wrestling club, known today as the DABC, one of the oldest amateur boxing clubs in Scotland. It is still going strong today. Hugh specialised in wrestling and won numerous trophies, eventually becoming champion of Northern Scotland. He also acted as an instructor, training many promising young wrestlers.

Hugh married a young Dundee girl, Marjory McGuigan, and they had two children, Alex and Elizabeth, before moving to Canada in 1912, taking only Alex with them. It seems likely that they left Elizabeth behind until they were settled in Canada. They lived at 297 Gertrude Avenue, Verdun in Montreal, where it is believed that Hugh worked with the railroad. On the outbreak of war in August 1914, he enlisted in the Princess Patricia's Canadian Light Infantry, newly formed in 1914, his regimental number being 1158. In October 1914, his No.3 Company became the first Canadian unit to serve on the Western Front.

Pte McKenzie fought with the regiment until 3 October 1915, when he was sent on a course by his Commanding Officer to train as a machine gunner. As a corporal, in May 1915 at St Eloi, he earned the Distinguished Conduct Medal, again with the Machine Gun Corps. The *London Gazette* citation reads:

> *For conspicuous gallantry. His machine gun having been blown up by a shell and the whole crew killed or wounded, Corporal McKenzie*

displayed the utmost coolness in stripping the wrecked gun of all undamaged parts and bringing them safely out of the trench, which by then had been absolutely demolished. Having no machine gun, he volunteered to carry messages to and from Brigade Headquarters under terrific fire and succeeded. His devotion to duty has always been most marked.

On 11 September 1915, he was promoted to Sergeant and in February 1916 was awarded the French Croix de Guerre for gallant and distinguished conduct in the field, the first machine gunner to receive this award. In September 1916, he was transferred to the 7th Canadian Machine Gun Company as Acting Company Sergeant Major, and on 28 January 1917 was promoted to Temporary Lieutenant.

During the night of 29/30 October 1917, the PPCLI, with Hugh McKenzie, were in action at Passchendaele as part of the 7th Brigade. With the 49th Edmontons, their task was to clear the pillboxes scattered across a narrow spur before pushing on to the north-west fringes of Passchendaele. McKenzie was in command of a small detachment of machine gunners accompanying the infantry. His orders were to move forward with the infantry, advancing in carefully dictated stages - at least that was the plan. In fact, the PPCLI were caught by enemy artillery and machine gun fire. Within two hours, almost every subaltern was either dead or wounded. In due course, they found themselves confronted by a heavily fortified pillbox on a relatively small mound, which, because of its elevated position, was able to rake the whole ridge with machine gun fire, causing severe casualties. They became bogged down at the foot of the ridge, sustaining evermore casualties, and McKenzie realised something needed to be done to restore impetus to their attack. Rising from a shell hole in which they were sheltering, McKenzie inspired his remaining men to charge towards the pillbox. Sadly, within 200 yards he was shot dead by a bullet in the head. Taking advantage of McKenzie's diversionary raid, another of his men, Sgt Harry Mullin MM got close to an enemy position near the pillbox and destroyed it with a hand grenade. Mullin then raced for the pillbox, climbed onto its roof and shot dead the machine gun crew before jumping down and accepting the surrender of ten prisoners. Nearby, another Canadian, Pte Cecil Kinross was performing equally valiant deeds and on 11 January 1918, the *London Gazette* announced the award of the Victoria Cross to Mullin and Kinross. Only on 13 February 1918 was the award of the Victoria Cross to McKenzie announced.

McKenzie was buried by his men near where he fell but his grave was subsequently destroyed by enemy artillery. He is remembered on the Menin Gate Memorial in Ypres.

From France, Hugh wrote regularly to a friend, Clement Hayward, in Canada and on one occasion asked Hayward to look up his wife and son. Hayward found that Hugh's wife had placed her son, Alex, in a home for young Protestant children in Montreal. Hayward wrote to Hugh but made no mention of what he had found. Shortly afterwards, Hugh was killed and Hayward went to Montreal to find Alex but learned that he had been collected by his mother. It seems that because of the hardship caused by the war, Marjorie found it necessary to place her son in the home.

After her father's death, Elizabeth moved from Scotland to Canada to be with her mother until her mother died. Alex stayed in Canada and fought in the Second World War. Shortly after his demobilisation, however, Alex was killed in a car accident. Elizabeth then moved back to Scotland, taking with her some of Hugh's medals. In 1955, her sister-in-law and three children were burned to death in a house fire in Amherstburg, Ontario. Hugh's Victoria Cross was lost in the fire. Elizabeth returned to Canada to live with her son in Windsor, Ontario. In 1970, following newspaper appeals, the PPCLI Regimental Museum made contact with her, shortly after she had returned from Scotland. Her father's DCM and Croix de Guerre had survived and she brought them back with her. The Regiment arranged for an official replacement Victoria Cross to be given to her, and she in turn donated this to the Canadian War Museum. It is currently on permanent loan to the PPCLI museum in Calgary, together with his DCM, Croix de Guerre and his service medals, alongside those of Mullin and Kinross.

The presentation of the replacement VC caused some controversy. A Mrs M.Pratt was writing a book on Victoria Cross winners and wrote to the PPCLI claiming that the Regiment had only two VC winners, McKenzie's belonging to the Machine Gun Corps. The Regiment disputed this allegation and Mrs Pratt consulted the War Office. The latter decreed that they considered his VC to be a PPCLI award. The Machine Gun Corps apparently concurred with this view, although some publications list him as both a PPCLI and a MGC winner of the Victoria Cross.